JET PIONEER:

A FIGHTER PILOT'S MEMOIR

marilyn

God bless,
Carl

JET PIONEER:

A FIGHTER PILOT'S MEMOIR

Carl G Schneider

Carl G. Schneider
Major General U.S. Air Force
(Retired)

Foreword by:
Dr. Buzz Aldrin
Astronaut, Gemini 12
& Apollo XI

With
Stan Corvin, Jr.
Author of
Vietnam Saga

ACKNOWLEDGMENTS:
Design Services: Melinda Martin - Martin Publishing Services.
PUBLISHING INFORMATION:
ICB - Scripture taken from the International Children's Bible®. Copyright © 1986, 1988,
1999 by Thomas Nelson All rights reserved.
NLT - New Living Translation, copyright © 1996, 2004, 2007 by Tyndale House Foundation.
All rights reserved.
NKJV - Scripture taken from the New King James Version®. Copyright © 1982 by Thomas
Nelson. All rights reserved.
NIV - Scripture quotations marked (NIV) are taken from the Holy Bible, New International
Version®, NIV®. Copyright © 1973, 1978, 1984, 2011 by Biblica, Inc.™ Used by permission
of Zondervan. All rights reserved worldwide. The "NIV" and "New International Version"
are trademarks registered in the United States Patent and Trademark Office by Biblica, Inc.™

ISBN: 978-0-9989222-0-1 (paperback), 978-0-9989222-1-8 (epub),
978-0-9989222-2-5 (hardback)

PUBLISHED BY: Southwestern Legacy Press
                8901 Tehama Ridge Parkway
                Suite 127-115
                Fort Worth, TX 76177
                www.swlegacypress.com

LIBRARY CATALOGING:
Names: Schneider, Carl G. (Carl G. Schneider)
Jet Pioneer: A Fighter Pilot's Memoir/Carl G. Schneider
190 pages 23cm × 15cm (9in. × 6 in.)
Description: Jet Pioneer is a memoir of the life and times of Carl G. Schneider, Major
General-USAF (Ret.), which covers his career from his entry into the U.S. Army Air Force as
an enlisted private to his retirement as a Major General thirty-two years later. The book also
contains numerous historic photos.
Key Words: Aviation, Combat, Flying, Korean War, Vietnam War

DEDICATION

During my service as a jet fighter pilot in the Korean War, twenty-two of my fellow pilots died, and three became POW's because of combat encounters or aircraft mishaps. They constituted seventy-eight percent of the total fighter group of thirty-two pilots. Most of them were in their early twenties. After returning home, to the United States, I visited many of their families and relived the pain of their loss again, as I had earlier felt it in the South Korea. That was a tough, emotional experience, but one of the most rewarding too!

This book is dedicated to those pilots and their families. Your sacrifice was not in vain (nor forgotten) and now over fifty million South Koreans enjoy a prosperous and thriving lifestyle and freedom, in part, because of your service.

May God bless you all, as He has blessed me so many times in my United States Air Force career and exciting life.

Major General Carl G. Schneider USAF (Ret.)

FOREWORD

DR. BUZZ ALDRIN, ASTRONAUT

I've known Major General Carl G. Schneider since the early 1950s, when we were young lieutenants stationed at Nellis Air Force Base in Las Vegas, Nevada, as F-86 Sabre instructor pilots. We both had just returned from flying combat missions in the Korean War and were responsible for training new jet fighter pilots in the F-86. Carl was twenty-three years old, and I was twenty-one.

Arriving in Bitburg, Germany, a few years later, I was assigned to the 22nd Fighter Squadron where we flew the F-100 Super Sabre. Carl was now a major and the squadron operations officer. I was a captain and was assigned as the "A" flight commander. We became friends, and our families were close, primarily because our apartment was next door to his and Elaine's. My son, Mike, and his daughter, Debi, who were both toddlers, frequently played together in a sandbox near the base apartment complex.

During one of our TDY gunnery exercise assignments to Wheelus Air Force Base in Tripoli, Libya, he and I spent a weekend on the Mediterranean beach snorkeling and shooting fish with our spear guns. I learned to scuba dive around that time, and little did I know how instrumental diving would be to my success as an astronaut. I became the first astronaut to train underwater to simulate the weightlessness of space, and because of this, I had five and one-half hours of successful spacewalking during my Gemini 12 mission in 1966.

One night the Russian "Sputnik" satellite slowly crossed the vast and starry sky. I wasn't as concerned about what it meant at that time because when you're a fighter pilot on five-minute alert carrying nuclear weapons, you've got other things on your mind. But my good friend, Ed White, whom I'd known since West Point, and who served with me in Korea, called to say he was applying to the astronaut program. I thought, "I can shoot better gunnery than Ed," so I decided to apply too, but I was turned down because I hadn't become a test pilot. My friend, Carl, had also encouraged me to apply to the astronaut program—further affirmation I needed to consider that career path seriously. I decided to continue my education at the Massachusetts Institute of Technology (MIT) since my father had received his doctorate in astronautics from there. Carl again encouraged me to do this, and his endorsement was extremely helpful in my being approved by the Department of Air Force for their graduate school. Three years later, I earned a ScD in astronautics, just like my father. In 1963, I was selected to participate in the third class of astronauts, and then on July 20, 1969, Neil Armstrong and I landed on the moon!

In 1948, Carl was assigned to Williams Air Force Base in Mesa, Arizona, to complete his advanced aviation cadet training. There, he flew the legendary P-51D propeller plane—a notoriously difficult airplane to fly with its massive engine up front limiting forward visibility and its tail dragging

FOREWORD

landing gear. Through his perseverance and hard work, Carl graduated at the top of his class, was commissioned a second lieutenant and earned his pilot wings. After graduation, Carl was assigned to Shaw Air Force Base in South Carolina, where he transitioned into the P-84—one of the first operational jet aircraft in the United States Air Force. So, Carl truly is a pioneer in the development of the U.S. jet air force.

Carl's book, *Jet Pioneer: A Fighter Pilot's Memoir,* tells the story, through his remarkable career, of the United States Air Force's post-World War II transition from propeller-driven airplanes to modern jet aircraft flying many times faster than the speed of sound or Mach 1. In many ways, his career could also be considered at "Mach 1" speed too since he began as an enlisted Army Air Force private in 1946 and rose to the rank of USAF Major General in 1976. Very few people have ever accomplished such a feat. His leadership and dedication to duty and love of flying are noteworthy and very commendable. Most Korean War veterans are now in their middle to late 80s, and their stories of bravery and dedication need to be told, so Major General Carl G. Schneider's story and this book will be a lasting legacy to his family, friends, and generations of aviation enthusiasts to come.

As the author of nine published books, I am honored and pleased to have been asked by Carl to write the foreword to his book, *Jet Pioneer: A Fighter Pilot's Memoir,* and highly recommend it. As pilots sometimes say, "I hope everything is CAVU *(Ceiling and Visibility Unlimited)* for you."

Dr. Buzz Aldrin
Astronaut, Gemini 12 & Apollo XI

...well done, good and faithful servant.
Mathew 25:21 NKJV

INTRODUCTION

On New Year's Day 2016, I made two resolutions. First was to write a book about my family and their origins and second was to write a book about my military career. With the publication of *Little House on the High Plains* and *Jet Pioneer: A Fighter Pilot's Memoir*, I have successfully fulfilled both resolutions. The books are now available in paperback on Amazon and e-books on Kindle.

Many people in the past have suggested I write a book about my thirty-two years of active duty service in the Air Force. I started as an enlisted private and progressed to the rank of Major General. This book relates my journey. Since the Civil War, very few men have risen through the ranks from private to general officer in all the United States military branches, and I'm proud to be among this elite group.

While chopping weeds in a cotton field as a young farm boy from West Texas during the Great Depression and Dust Bowl era, I had an "epiphany." My life's work was to be a fighter pilot. The event started me on an amazing journey, which changed the course of my life from what I would've been—a West Texas farmer—to an Air Force officer and pilot traveling the world.

In the dedication to this book, I acknowledge the "ultimate sacrifice" of many of my friends, flying buddies, and colleagues who died while serving their country. We were all very young, in our early twenties, and believed we were invincible. Of course, that was not true, and a staggering number of young pilots died.

Aviation in general and flying jet aircraft specifically, is inherently a dangerous occupation. In peacetime, weather-related crashes, maintenance problems, equipment failures and pilot error are usually the main causes of death among flyers. During wartime conflicts (in my case, the Korean and Vietnam Wars), fatalities among pilots dramatically increased because of the additional dangers of enemy aircraft, ground fire from small arms, antiaircraft weapons, and later surface-to-air missiles.

This memoir is for the most part chronologically accurate with each chapter being written in essay style about a specific period in my life and the surrounding events. I have included many anecdotes and personal stories to add "flavor" to the chapters and bring the reader along metaphorically in the back seat for the "ride." Some stories are funny, but most are serious because war and combat flying are dangerous and deadly.

Because I was actively involved in flying many combat missions both in Korea and Vietnam, I initially experienced mild PTSD symptoms of flashbacks, sleeplessness, and anxiety after returning home. Post-traumatic stress disorder (PTSD), a term coined after the Vietnam War, can develop when a person is exposed to a severe traumatic event such as a violent episode in war. However, trauma-related symptoms are not a new thing and have been documented since the time of the ancient Greeks.

I have been saddened by the loss of many friends and comrades over the years. However, I am eternally grateful for the inner strength I found from my faith in Almighty God—the God of all hope—who has given me a positive mental attitude. Both have served me well over the past eighty-eight years.

Finally, I want this book to serve as a legacy for my family members who read it with the expectation that it will be passed down to future generations of the extended Schneider clan. Also, I believe the book can inspire young people to overcome the obstacles they will inevitably encounter in life and achieve great success despite, perhaps, coming from humble beginnings.

I sincerely hope that you enjoy reading *Jet Pioneer: A Fighter Pilot's Memoir.*

Carl G. Schneider, Major General
United States Air Force (Retired)

JET PILOT

When I have watched you leave the world behind
To soar through endless skies on silvered wings
Beyond the reach of petty man-made things
In search of truth, on earth left undefined;
When I have glimpsed the joy of all your kind
Who dart among the clouds as youthful kings
Surmounting billowed mist, you cut the strings
Of worldly care, which makes the earthbound blind.
And as I gaze into your dancing eyes
When your reluctant feet are on the sod,
I look into a heart still with the sky
Where gladness of a moment never dies,
Remembering short whispered talks with God
And this, the Golden Dream of men to fly!

—Author Unknown

TABLE OF CONTENTS

PROLOGUE

On December 1, 1978, while walking to my car and carrying a small box of personal items from my office, I instinctively looked up when I suddenly heard the familiar roar of two F-4 Phantom jet fighters flying in close formation as they passed overhead. They were entering the traffic pattern for landing at Wright-Patterson Air Force Base, in Dayton, Ohio. The sound of their engines reminded me of when I was leading a group of eight F-100s across the North Atlantic, and we became lost, but finally found our destination in the Azores just as our fuel ran out.

Lost! I can't believe it. Here we are lost over the North Atlantic with no navigational aids or radios. Flying at five hundred knots and no alternate landing field in which to land.

If we have to bail out, because we've run out of fuel, no one will ever find us. The search area will extend from the eastern coast of Newfoundland to the West Coast of Portugal, and we'll die from hypothermia within thirty minutes in the frigid water.

I grimly looked over at my wingman. We had lost radio communication with each other and were using hand signals to indicate that we could not transmit or receive over our radios. Making matters worse, my navigational aids were not working properly, and I had to rely solely upon my magnetic compass to maintain the easterly heading to our refueling stop in the Azores.

Earlier that morning, we had departed the United States and were flying at 35,000 feet to Lajes Field in the Azores. Upon our departure, the destination weather was forecast to be overcast with a ceiling of fifteen hundred feet and three miles visibility; however, a cold front had moved into the area since we had departed Newfoundland and dropped the ceiling and visibility down to three hundred feet and one mile. We had just completed the worldwide gunnery competition at Nellis Air Force Base in Las Vegas and were flying back to Bitburg, Germany.

I was leading the first ferry flight of four airplanes in a group of eight F-100 Super Sabre fighter jets going to the Azores to refuel. Two flights stayed at Harmon Air Force Base, Newfoundland, to correct several maintenance problems.

After several hours of "dead reckoning" navigation—figuring time, distance, and heading—my handheld E6B flight computer (nicknamed the "whiz wheel" and resembling a circular slide rule), indicated that we would use up all of our fuel approximately ten minutes before we reached our refueling point. When I looked at the instrument panel, my fuel gauge showed that I had minimum fuel left, and I thought the tanks were nearly empty. Also, with no local altimeter settings being provided by the airfield tower, we really had no idea about our actual height above ground level (AGL) once we descended into the dark clouds below.

I had landed at the field before and knew there was a small mountain a few miles west of the runway. Suddenly, I saw the barely visible mountain peak jutting out of the clouds and knew we were only a few miles south of our destination. Waving at my wingman, I took my right hand and excitedly pointed down, indicating we were going to begin a fast descent into the thick cloud cover below.

As I entered the dark overcast skies, I lost sight of his F-100 flying close beside me off my right wingtip. Within a few seconds, we broke out of the clouds, and I saw the runway ahead. There were no aircraft in the traffic pattern, so we made a circling approach and safely touched down on the 10,000-foot runway.

As I taxied to the airport terminal and base operations, my engine abruptly flamed out (quit) from fuel starvation, and the jet quietly and slowly rolled to a stop on the taxiway. My wingman's engine also quit at the same time, and we sat there until vehicles called "tugs" came and towed us to the refueling area. All of the other aircraft landed safely. After repairs were made to our radios and navigational aids, and we refueled, we departed the next day for Bitburg.

Being lost over the North Atlantic Ocean with no communications or ability to navigate had been a harrowing and nerve-wracking experience; however, we survived the encounter, and I was forever grateful that my small flight group of eight F-100s and I had been spared a watery grave.

My retirement ceremony, which had been held at the National Museum of the United States Air Force, was over and I was leaving for the long drive to Arizona, where I planned to live permanently. After thirty-two years of active duty in the USAF, I had achieved my goal to become a fighter pilot. As I sat in my car before leaving the parking lot, I felt a strong sense of nostalgia thinking about how it all started long ago. My journey began with the sound of a very different airplane, in a very different time, at a place which now exists only in my heart!

...Listen to my teachings. Hear what I say. I will speak using stories. I will tell you things that have been secret ...
Psalm 78:1-4 (ICB)

A FARM BOY 1937

When I was nine years old and chopping weeds in the middle of my family's cotton field while warily watching a nearby whirling dust devil, my younger brother, Clyde, and I suddenly heard the distant sound of an airplane engine. Putting my hand to my forehead to shade my eyes from the intensely blazing West Texas sun, I soon saw a single-engine biplane approaching. As it neared us, the plane began to perform several aerobatic maneuvers directly overhead.

Mesmerized by the wild gyrations and impressed with the flying skill of the pilot, I turned to Clyde and said, "Someday that's what I'm going to do. I'm going to be a fighter pilot!"

He grinned at me childishly and said, "Then I'm going to be a pilot too."

Living and working on my grandfather's Kerlin's and Schneider's homestead farms in Ralls, Texas, my two brothers and three sisters and I were reared during The Great Depression and the Dustbowl period. While the era was difficult for most of the town folks, the times were never as bad for our family as John Steinbeck's novel and subsequent movie *The Grapes of Wrath* depicted.

For years, many American farmers had overplanted and poorly managed their crop rotations. Between 1930 and 1936, when severe drought conditions prevailed across much of western America's Plains, blowing clouds of dust were created. High winds turned the soil to dust, and large dark clouds could be seen across the horizon in Texas, Oklahoma, Kansas, Nebraska, Colorado, and New Mexico.

Topsoil was carried by the ton from barren fields across hundreds of miles of plains in the driest regions of the country. Black Sunday, April 14, 1935, a day when winds reached sustained speeds of sixty miles per hour, an associated press reporter was prompted to coin the term "dust bowl" for the occurrences.

The agricultural depression was a major factor in the country's Great Depression as farmers defaulted on their bank loans, credit dried up, and banking institutions closed across the country. Throughout the 1930s, more than a million acres of land were adversely affected by the dust bowl, thousands of farmers lost their livelihoods and property, and mass migration patterns began to emerge as farmers left rural America in search of work in urban areas. This migration added to unemployment woes, stressed relief and benefits programs and created social strife in many large American cities.[1]

Because of the ever-present dust and lack of rain, we didn't have "two nickels to rub together" (West Texas jargon for having no cash) and did not "make" (harvest) a crop for seven years. We had plenty of food and ate well-prepared and nourishing meals consisting mostly of fresh garden vegetables, chicken-fried steak, ground beef, cornbread, and pinto beans (which I still enjoy today).

We butchered our own hogs and cows (not our milk cows), and my mother had a "truck" garden that provided all our vegetables. She also raised broiler chickens to fry and laying pullets, so we had an abundance of fresh eggs. While we were growing up, we worked hard but were a very happy family that laughed frequently, played well together and had a lot of fun.

Occasionally, when one of us misbehaved, our mother would administer our punishment in the form of "peach tree tea." The offending child had to go to the backyard and cut a peach tree limb about two feet long and as thick as your thumb. Then our mother used the switch on our rear ends or legs. Usually, only one session was necessary to improve our attitude and behavior. Our feelings were hurt more than our anatomy, but the switching was an effective form of corporal punishment, mainly because we felt ashamed because we had done something to upset our mother. My oldest sister and I were usually the "guilty parties" because we were held to a higher standard than our four younger siblings and were supposed to demonstrate an example of good behavior at all times.

We attended church services on Sundays and frequently participated in social gatherings called "potluck" suppers there with our neighbors. The era was a kinder, gentler, simpler time and I am now filled with feelings of melancholy as I think about those days.

My family moved to Plainview, located in Hale County in West Texas, where I attended high school. One of my classmates was Jimmy Dean, who dropped out of school to join the USAF to help his family financially. A few years later, at the age of twenty- two, he began a singing and acting career and became famous. His song "Big Bad John" was a country music and national hit and is still occasionally played on the radio.

In 1969, he and his brother, Don, started the Jimmy Dean Sausage Company, and he became the spokesman for the company's products on television, where he had his own variety show. In 2008, two years before his death, Jimmy Dean donated one million dollars to Wayland Baptist University in Plainview, the largest single donation ever made to the institution. I was proud of my former classmate.

My brother, Clyde, and I joined the local Civil Air Patrol and began to read everything we could find about flying and airplanes. Clyde saved enough money to take a few flying lessons in an Aeronca Champion airplane, and he actually soloed after two hours and fifteen minutes of instruction. I flew my first airplane, a T-6 "Texan" trainer, a few years later when I started pilot training at Randolph Field in San Antonio.

Clyde graduated from Texas Technological College in Lubbock, Texas. After he had joined the USAF, he completed multiengine pilot training and flew B-25 bombers at Reece AFB, a few miles west of town. While he was in flight school, he met his future wife, Martha. They were married immediately after he finished his training and was commissioned as a second lieutenant.

After graduation, he first flew large cargo planes in the United States beginning with the Fairchild C-119, which was an American military transport aircraft developed after World War II and designed to carry cargo, personnel, litter patients, and mechanized equipment. The aircraft also dropped cargo and troops by parachute. The cargo-hauling ability and unusual twin-boom design earned it the nickname "Flying Boxcar."

Later, in Japan and Korea, he flew Curtis C-46s and Douglas C-47s. The Curtiss C-46 Commando was a cargo aircraft derived from the Curtiss pressurized high-altitude airliner design and was used as a military transport during World War II by the United States Army Air Forces.

The Douglas C-47 Skytrain was a military transport aircraft developed from the civilian Douglas DC-3 airliner and was used extensively by the Allies during World War II. The plane remains in service with various military operators to the present day.

In 1949, the C-47 was used extensively during the Berlin Blockade airlift where hundreds of American cargo planes flew through narrow corridors of airspace before landing at Templehof Airport in downtown Berlin. Each of the planes delivered three and a half tons of food, water, milk, and coal for heating because the Russians had closed all access roads to the city to starve the inhabitants into becoming Soviet subjects. The blockade lasted for approximately eleven months and ended after the Russians failed to intimidate the Berliners.

On June 26, 1963, U.S. President John F. Kennedy addressed a huge crowd of Berliners gathered at the Brandenburg Gate. There he made his famous comment, "Two thousand years ago, the proudest boast was *civis Romanus sum* (I am a Roman citizen). Today, in the world of freedom, the proudest boast is *Ich bin ein Berliner* (I am a Berliner).[2]

Carl's Home in Plainview, TX

Carl at 17

Carl on Horseback

MY ENLISTMENT

"I want to be a fighter pilot," I boldly told the old sergeant when I walked into the recruiting office in Plainview, Texas. While he held a sheaf of papers in his hand, he looked at me and, after walking to his desk, said, "Just sign here, son, and we'll get you right in." The date was September 18, 1946, and I was eighteen years old. I had finished one year of college at Texas Technological College in Lubbock on an agricultural scholarship from Sears Roebuck and Company; however, funds were not available for further schooling, so I decided to join the U.S. Army Air Force.

A few days after my enlistment, several other recruits and I boarded a bus and rode to Goodfellow AFB, in San Angelo, Texas. After spending the night, we were sworn into the U.S. Army Air Force the following morning. The next day, we rode buses to Lackland AFB in San Antonio. San Antonio was the biggest town I'd been to since I was fourteen years old when my thirteen-year-old brother Clyde and I rode to Fort Worth, Texas, on a motorcycle we had bought and rebuilt.

As we arrived at Lackland, we drove past several large groups of World War II veterans sitting on fences, who were processing out of the service, and they mockingly yelled very loudly, "You'll be sorry!"

We were assigned to old wooden barracks in a basic training company, and a drill sergeant began immediately having us march in formation. The classes we took were about the Army Air Force history and other relevant military subjects. We marched everywhere and did a lot of athletics and physical training. A few days after we arrived, we hiked thirteen miles around Camp Bullis, a bivouac area north of San Antonio. While we were in formation, one of the straps broke on my fully loaded backpack, and I had to carry the pack in my arms for about ten back-breaking miles!

Basic training lasted eight weeks. After the second week, we were given a pass for Saturday night and went into downtown San Antonio where I had my first T-bone steak. On our farm in West Texas, my family couldn't often afford steak, while I was growing up, and when we did, we had to share with everybody.

I enjoyed basic training. I got to shower every day, which was a luxury because the barracks had indoor plumbing which my family home did not have. The Air Force training, although somewhat physically difficult, took place primarily in classrooms and was a lot easier than working on my family's farm.

On the weekends, we'd go to downtown San Antonio to the River Walk, which was not as large and extensive as today, and stroll around. However, the restaurants were too expensive for us to afford on our meager pay. Hearing music playing one weekend, several friends and I went to the Arneson River Theater and sat on the grass terraces while watching traditional Mexican dancers perform. The women wore long, brightly colored dresses, and the men wore tight-fitting silver-brocaded pants, vests, and large sombreros.

Enlisted AAF Private

REMOTE CONTROL B-29
TURRET MECHANIC

After basic training completion, many of us boarded a train for Lowry Field in Denver, Colorado. The grueling, circuitous, thirty-six hour trip by troop train with no air conditioning and only hard wooden benches on which to sit wound through New Orleans and St. Louis before we got to Colorado. The windows were open for ventilation, which caused the diesel fumes and smoke and soot to blow in and cover our uniforms and faces with a thick layer of grime.

Lowry AFB (Lowry Field 1938-1948) was a United States Army Air Forces (USAAF) training base during World War II and a United States Air Force (USAF) training base during the Cold War, Lowry served as the initial 1955-1958 site of the U.S. Air Force Academy. Lowry Field was named for 2nd Lieutenant Francis Lowry, the only Colorado pilot killed in combat during WWI.

A vacant sanatorium building, which had been established as a tuberculosis hospital in 1904, was used as the first military school until the permanent facility was completed in Colorado Springs. The sanatorium's main building became the Army post's headquarters, and the largest single barracks, which housed 3,200 men, was completed in mid-1940. Lowry began training for Boeing B-29 Super Fortress pilot qualification and for B-29 operational crew readiness in 1943.[3]

We finally unloaded from the train at Lowry's railroad station. A sergeant rounded us up, put us in a company formation and marched us to our new barracks. The first day on the base, we went through a classification process, and I was assigned as an automotive mechanic. I told a buddy I didn't want to go to auto mechanic school. He was a couple of years older and had one year of ROTC, so he said, "Why don't you go over to the personnel office and see if you can talk to someone about changing your training school."

The personnel office was a big room featuring a desk square in the middle and a lone sergeant sitting at it reading some paperwork. When I walked over to the front of his desk, he said, "What do you want, son?"

I replied, "Sir—"

Quickly jumping up, he yelled loudly in my face, "Don't call me sir. I'm a sergeant!"

I answered, "Yes, sergeant. I don't want anything to do with automobiles or trucks because I want to work on airplanes."

He walked to a filing cabinet, pulled out some files and paperwork, looked through the stack and said, "I've got one slot for a B-29 remote-controlled turret mechanic. It's the toughest course we've got here, and many of the students wash out before it's finished. It's a six months' course, but if you graduate, you'll be promoted from a private, which you are right now, to a corporal."

As quickly as my mouth would open, I said, "I'll take it, sergeant." I graduated from the course at the top of my class and was promoted to corporal.

Once my training was completed, I was given Christmas leave and went home to Plainview, Texas, for the holidays. I hitched a ride in his 1939 Ford with a friend of mine, who was going to his home in Lubbock, Texas, about thirty miles from Plainview.

We were anxious to get home and see our families, but a blinding snowstorm and arctic cold front had moved in from the north, so it took us many hours to reach our homes. It's a good thing that Ford had a working heater, or we would've been frozen for Christmas.

After the holidays, I returned to Lowry and learned that aviation cadet pilot training was now accepting applications. The next morning, I was the first one in line at the cadet examining center. When I was inside, a captain came up to me and in a gruff voice said, "What do you want?"

I confidently said, "I want to go to flight school."

He looked me up and down and then said, "Go over to the testing center and take all the tests."

I did as he ordered and made top scores on all the exams, primarily because of what I'd learned in the Civil Air Patrol back home and the voluminous amount of reading about flying I had already done. Returning to the examining center, I approached the captain. Friendlier now, he told me, "The flight school will begin in June 1947, so go to your next assignment, and you'll be notified when to report to the school."

Shortly after that, I was transferred to Roswell Field in New Mexico for my first enlisted airman's job.

ROSWELL FIELD/WALKER AFB

In the late 1940s and early 1950s, many bases changed their names to honor heroes of Air Force history. This was in keeping with the newly established USAF as an independent defense agency on September 18, 1947. Accordingly, Roswell Field became Walker AFB on January 13, 1948—named for Brigadier General Kenneth N. Walker, a native of New Mexico.

Two bomber units were assigned to Roswell/Walker—the more famous one was the 509th Bomber Wing. Its 393rd Bomb Squadron was the only combat unit ever to have dropped atomic bombs on enemy targets. On August 6, one of the wing's B-29s, the "Enola Gay," piloted by the wing commander, Col. Paul W. Tibbetts, Jr., dropped an atomic bomb on Hiroshima, Japan. Three days later, a B-29, "Bock's Car," piloted by Major Charles W. Sweeney, dropped a differently configured atomic bomb on Nagasaki. These two missions quickly caused the Japanese Empire to surrender, and the war ended. The unit returned to the United States at Roswell Field on November 6, 1945. Assigned to the Strategic Air Command (SAC) upon that command's activation, the unit provided the nucleus for an atomic strike. During the summer of 1946, the 509th participated in atomic tests in the Marshall Islands.[4]

I was assigned as a B-29 armament mechanic at Roswell Field. A few weeks later, I went into the cadet training center and spoke to the captain who was the officer in charge (OIC). After examining my file, he said, "Everything looks in order; however, your audiometer (hearing) test is missing. You can get one at Kirtland Field in Albuquerque, New Mexico. There's a C-47 at base operations that's going there in a few minutes. Run back to the barracks, get an overnight bag of clothes and go to the airplane. I'll call right now and get your name on the manifest." I ran to pack a small bag, showed up at the plane and got on just before its departure. I thought the captain would notify my company first sergeant about my leaving; however, he didn't.

We arrived at Kirtland that afternoon where I took another hearing test and passed it. Afterward, I called my aunt and uncle, who lived nearby and spent the night with them. The next morning, I went back to base operations thinking I was going to catch a plane back to Roswell Field. "No airplanes today, son. Maybe tomorrow," the operations sergeant told me.

I went back to my aunt and uncle's and spent the night again. The next morning, I returned to base operations and learned the only flight to Roswell was in two days. Somewhat worried, I went back to my family's house and waited a couple of days until the C-47 arrived. I got on it and flew back to Roswell Field.

When I walked into the orderly room of my unit, the scowling first sergeant jumped up, mad as he could be, and said, "Son, you have been AWOL for four days! Luckily, your orders for aviation cadet training came in while you were gone. I'm giving you two hours to get off this base, or you'll be court-martialed. I'll be standing at the front gate to make sure you leave!"

I ran to the barracks, gathered all my gear and went to the personnel center, supply room, and other base offices to clear out from my current assignment. I got to the front gate just as the two hours expired; I saw the first sergeant standing there with crossed arms and tapping one foot. Breathing hard, I walked out to the nearby highway and hitchhiked five hundred miles to Randolph Field in San Antonio, Texas.

B-29 509 Bomb Group

PRIMARY AND BASIC AVIATION CADET TRAINING

Two days later, after arriving at the Randolph Field main gate carrying my big duffel bag, I walked up to an MP and told him I was reporting for aviation cadet training. "Son, you are already late, and the cadet barracks are on the southeast side of the base; but, don't you dare cut through the officer's area to get to it." I ran around the perimeter of the base with the heavy duffel bag to get to my cadet company area and reported to the orderly room as an official aviation cadet.

Since it opened in 1931, Randolph has been a flight-training facility for the United States Army Air Corps, the USAAF, and the USAF during its entire existence. Randolph AFB was named after Captain William Randolph, a native of Austin, Texas, who was on the base-naming committee at the time of his death in a crash. Randolph serves as headquarters for the Air Education and Training Command (AETC) as well as the Air Force Personnel Center (AFPC) and is known as "The Showplace of the Air Force" because of the Spanish colonial, revival-style architecture in which all structures including hangars were constructed. The world famous symbol of the base is a large water tower atop Building 100, which houses the headquarters of Randolph's major flying unit, the 12th Flying Training Wing (12 FTW). With its distinctive architecture, the wing's headquarters has come to be known throughout the Air Force as "the Taj Mahal," or simply "The Taj."[5]

We had a cadet club on the base and another one in the Gunter Hotel in downtown San Antonio. On the weekend, the Gunter was a swinging place with lots of local girls coming to meet cadets and dance.

The Gunter Hotel opened on November 20, 1909, on the site of the earlier Mahncke Hotel. There has been a hotel or inn on the same site since 1837. The eight-story, 301-room hotel was built by the San Antonio Hotel Company and named for Jot Gunter, a local rancher and real estate developer who was one of its financiers. For many decades, the Gunter was the largest building in San Antonio. The large insurance company, United Services Automobile Association (USAA), was formed based on a meeting of twenty-five United States Army officers on June 22, 1922, at the Gunter Hotel to discuss the procurement of reliable and economical auto insurance for its proposed customers.

For the first week, we marched all day. The second week, we started academic classes and began to fly. Our schedule was to have classroom instruction for a half day and then fly for a half day. We flew the AT-6 "Texan," manufactured by North American Aviation, which was a tandem two-seat, single-engine, advanced trainer aircraft. The plane had a loud, six hundred horsepower radial engine, a retractable main landing gear, and a top speed of 208 mph. My instructor was a very good pilot, and since I had driven fast motorcycles, tractors, and cars, flying came easy for me.

One day when I was practicing spins, my instructor told me, "If you don't recover from the spin on a cardinal heading, I'm going to recommend you for a check ride." The consequence of failing a check ride was to wash out of the flight program.

I replied, "Sir, no one ever told me I was supposed to do that." From then on, every time I recovered from a spin, my headings were 090, 180, 270 or 360 degrees—all cardinal headings.

Our takeoffs and landings took place from grass strips in a large open field, and I enjoyed taxiing the airplane very fast. Once, when I was going too fast, my instructor pilot said, "Mister, I think you caught a wing tip when you landed, so get out and check to see if there's any damage."

Knowing that I hadn't, I reluctantly said, "Yes, sir," and obeyed his direct order.

Then he yelled at me, "Hang on to the wing tip until I tell you to let go!" Revving the engine, he began taxiing very fast around the perimeter of the grass practice field while I hung on, running as fast as I could. Finally, we arrived at the paved parking ramp. I was wearing a seat type parachute with heavy straps over my shoulders and through my legs. All the blisters from the straps chafing my skin took three weeks to heal; however, from then on, I never taxied too fast. I had learned my lesson the hard and painful way.

All the instructors were very good, and most had been World War II fighter pilots. After about two hundred hours of training, I completed my primary and basic flight-school instruction and was ready to move on to the next phase of flight training.

Randolph Field Taj Mahal Building with Training Aircraft

Audaces fortuna iuvat (Latin)—Virgil
Fortune Favors the Bold!

ADVANCED AVIATION CADET TRAINING

After basic aviation training, my name was posted on a list of cadets being sent to the multiengine course of flight instruction, which meant I was to be flying bombers. Going to my tactical (TAC) officer, I said, "Sir, I want to be a fighter pilot, not a bomber pilot."

He angrily replied, "Cadet, you'll go where you are told."

I said, "Then, sir, I'd like permission to talk to the Commandant of Cadets."

After receiving permission to meet with the Commandant, I walked into the Colonel's office, saluted smartly and, standing at attention at his desk, declared, "Sir, I'm not going to multiengine school."

He jumped up out of his chair and proceeded to chew me out for several minutes about my attitude. He was red in the face, and I thought he was going to have a heart attack, but suddenly he stopped talking, angrily stormed out of the room and slammed the door shut.

In a few minutes, he walked back into the room and said, "Sit down, son. You've got more guts than any kid I've ever seen, and you've got spirit, so I'm going to waive the multiengine orders and send you to fighter pilot school. We need people like you in fighters."

The reason I was chosen for multiengine training and bombers instead of jets was that at six foot one, I was taller than most fighter pilots. The cockpits of the first jet fighters were very small, and the rudder pedals were so close to the seat, my knees were bent almost to my chest.

The colonel who changed my orders clearly violated Air Force regulations. That was my first lesson in an officer having the "guts" to go against established regulations if it made sense—a lesson that I frequently practiced during my career.

In a few days, my orders came in transferring me to Williams AFB in Mesa, Arizona. Several other cadets were going there too, so we piled into one of their cars that had a trailer hitched to it to carry our bags. We planned to drive straight through. On the west side of El Paso, we came around a curve near Deming, New Mexico, and hit a flooded area of highway that looked like the Pacific Ocean and stalled out the car engine.

A thunderstorm had dumped several inches of rain in the desert and flooded the entire area. The next morning the water level had receded, and the engine had dried out enough so that we could start it. Slowly limping into Deming, New Mexico, we had the car repaired and then continued to Arizona.

There's an old joke about Deming: The doctor says, "You've got only one more day to live. Where do you want to go?"

The patient says, "I want to go to Deming, New Mexico."

Puzzled, the doctor asks, "Why in the world do you want to go to Deming?"

The patient answers, "I was there once, and it was the longest day of my life."

February 1948, we arrived at Williams AFB and started academic classes to learn to fly the famous P-51D World War II fighter. Every spare moment before flying the aircraft, I sat in the cockpit memorizing where all the instruments were located and visualizing the various aspects of flying including engine starting, taxiing out, run up procedures, takeoffs, stall series, and all the acrobatic maneuvers such as lazy eights and chandelles. I had over thirty hours in the cockpit before taking my first flight.

After a week, I began to fly in the back seat, which only had an airspeed indicator, altimeter, magnetic compass, rudder pedals, stick, and throttle. With an instructor pilot, I flew to auxiliary fields around Phoenix and practiced takeoffs and landings called "touch-and-go" in the aircraft. Sitting in the backseat, I couldn't see much in front of me, so I had trouble "rounding out" on my landings, which resulted in me bouncing and "ricocheting" down the runway. After a while, my instructor said, "Carl, I don't think you can land this aircraft, so I'm going to have to put you up for a check ride!"

I replied, "Sir, if I sit up front, I can land the plane with no problem."

We taxied back to base operations, and he told me to sit in the shade under the wing and wait for the check ride pilot to come out. After a while, an instructor pilot, who was a captain, came out and began asking me questions about where I was from and about my family—trying to calm me down because I was obviously nervous.

Finally, he said, "What seems to be the problem?"

I answered, "Sir, I'm sitting down so low in the back seat I can't see the runway to round out, but if I'm sitting in the front seat, I can."

Standing there a moment, he asked, "Do you think you can fly this airplane from the front seat?"

"Yes, sir. I know I can!" I emphatically answered.

Patting me on the shoulder, he said, "Then get up front and go fly." Turning around, he walked back into base operations. That was the end of my check ride.

After that, my training consisted of learning to fly in formation, going on cross-country flights and various aspects of fighter tactics. I did well, graduated at the top of my class and was commissioned a second lieutenant.

At graduation, the instructors told us we were going to be the pilots to perform the flyby at the graduation ceremony. We organized everything, took off and flew over all the families that attended the graduation. Then we landed, rushed to change into class "A" uniforms, attended the ceremony and pinned on our coveted pilot's wings.

My mom, dad, and sisters, Joyce and JoAnn, came to the graduation and stayed with my aunt and uncle, who lived outside of Phoenix. After returning home to Texas, I had thirty days' leave and enjoyed visiting my old Texas Tech roommates in Lubbock, while wearing my new uniform and wings. After my leave, I reported to my new permanent change of station (PCS) in South Carolina.

Carl as 2nd Lieutenant

2nd Lt. Schneider and buddies by P-51D

SHAW AIR FORCE BASE

S haw AFB is located approximately eight miles northwest of Sumter, South Carolina. The base is named in honor of a pilot, First Lieutenant Ervin David Shaw. Lieutenant Shaw, a Sumter County native, was one of the first Americans to fly combat missions in World War I. He was assigned to the Royal Air Force 48th Squadron as a member of the Royal Canadian Air Service. Shaw died after three enemy aircraft attacked his fighter aircraft while he was returning from a reconnaissance mission on 9 July 1918.[6]

One morning, I was in squadron operations when the operations officer walked up to me and said, "Let's get you checked out in a jet." He gave me a questionnaire of about fifteen to twenty questions regarding the F-84 flight characteristics and a copy of the Dash–1 airplane operating manual that had all the answers in it. I spent the next two hours studying information about how to start the engine, take-off speed, gear up speed, landing approach speeds, local operating procedures and traffic pattern facts, etc. At 1100 hours, he came back and asked, "Are you finished?"

"Yes, sir, I am," I answered.

"Then let's go get some lunch, and when we come back, we will go out to the aircraft, and you can look at it," he said.

Returning to base ops after lunch, the instructor pilot said, "Go get your parachute and helmet and meet me out at the aircraft."

"Sir, I don't have a helmet—just the leather one I used when I was flying P-51s," I replied.

"You can use my helmet until the new shipment arrives," he said.

We went out to the aircraft and walked around it performing the preflight inspection. A ladder was brought to the side of the airplane, and the instructor said, "Go ahead and climb in and start the aircraft."

"Sir, I've never started a jet engine before," I hesitatingly said.

"Go ahead and climb in, and I'll start it for you," the instructor replied.

The F-84 was a single-seat jet airplane since we had no twin-seated jets at that time. After I sat down and strapped in, the instructor climbed the ladder, reached inside the cockpit and started the engine with me sitting there. I was so scared my knees were shaking badly, and I could barely hold the brakes down. Fortunately, the jet took so much power to move that I just sat there. Patting me on the shoulder, the instructor said, "You'll be okay. Now go fly!"

Applying engine power, I taxied to the end of the runway and called the tower, which cleared me for takeoff. After departure, I flew several miles away from the base, climbed to 30,000 feet and practiced chandelles (a maneuver where the pilot combines an 180-degree turn with a climb), stalls, high "G" (gravity) turns, and then returned to Shaw where I practiced several touch-and-go landings. *Boy, this is a piece of cake compared to flying the P-51D tail dragger.*

Landing for the final time, I taxied back to base operations, parked the aircraft, slid the canopy back and climbed down the ladder that had been brought out to me. I walked into the building, and the instructor saw me and said, "Well, I see that you survived!" as he began to laugh. That completed my entire check out for flying my first jet—basically, "kick the tire and light the fire."

Several months later at a pilots' briefing, the operations officer walked in and said, "I need a bachelor for a six months' 'dirty detail.' Any of you guys stupid enough to volunteer?"

Instantly raising my hand, I enthusiastically said, "Yes, sir, I'll do it!"

While I was in basic training at Lackland AFB, one of the guys in the training flight was a corporal by the name of Schmidt who was from New Jersey. He told us, "Youse guys, don't never volunteer for nuttin!" After telling us that, I decided that I would volunteer for everything if asked.

Looking around the briefing room, the operations officer said "Eat your hearts out, guys. Carl's going to New York City and ferry new F-84s from the Republic airplane factory on Long Island to air bases all around the country. He's going to live in the Hotel Pennsylvania in downtown Manhattan."

A few days later, I received my new orders. After flying to New York, I checked in at the Republic manufacturing plant and met with the old, heavyset civilian who was responsible for sending the new jets out to their assigned bases.

Sitting in his office, I asked, "Sir, what are my duties?"

He answered, "Lieutenant, go ahead and check into the hotel and wait for me to call you. Once we have an airplane that is completed and is test flown, I'll let you know and send a car to pick you up. Then I'll tell you where it is supposed to go. You'll come on out here and fill out all the paperwork then file a flight plan to Texas, California, or wherever the airplane's going.

"While you're waiting in Manhattan, if you want to go to any Broadway shows, just let me know, and I'll call and get tickets for you, and they'll hold them at the "will call" window. To pay for them, just sign as Republic Aircraft Company when you pick them up. If you want to eat at any of the downtown restaurants, go ahead and do so and just sign the check with our company name and we will pick up the tab."

Then I asked, "When I deliver the jet, how am I supposed to get back here?"

Reaching into a desk drawer, he pulled out a thick pad of blank first-class airline tickets and handed them to me saying, "Take these with you and after you've delivered the airplane, check the return airline flight schedules and fill out one of these tickets and you can fly back here. As a bachelor, you probably have girlfriends all around the country, so if you want to go see them, that will be okay too. Just try to be back here ten days after you have delivered the plane."

In those days, there were no civilian jet airliners, so a jet fighter pilot was like an "astronaut" and very admired by all the girls who were called stewardesses at that time (later, they were called flight attendants). Many times, they eagerly accepted my dinner date invitation when we arrived at our destination.

Arriving back at Shaw Air Force Base, I was not a very popular guy for a while because of the "cushy" job I'd had for the previous six months. Eventually, that changed and I became a part of the "brotherhood" of pilots. Ferrying the jets around the country had been a grand adventure for a young second lieutenant.

Heading to Eglin Air Force Base in Florida for gunnery training one morning, we cleared the runway and began our turn out of the traffic pattern when my new flight leader, flying in the F-84 next to me, rolled over, inverted and crashed into the ground. The accident board said that his flight controls broke upon takeoff rendering the aircraft uncontrollable. I circled around the dense black column of smoke coming from his burning airplane, waited until the next flight took off and then joined up with them. We flew down to Eglin and spent a few days firing our fifty-caliber machine guns on the gunnery ranges located there. Then we returned to Shaw. There was a funeral ceremony for the pilot who had been killed a few days earlier. Within the first year, six pilots, unfortunately, died due to defective wings breaking off and other structural defects.

Initially, we didn't have any proper helmets to wear, so we'd go to a local sporting goods store and buy a football helmet big enough to wear over our leather flight helmets with headphones, and we'd pull the straps down under the chin. Several months later, our unit received newly designed plastic helmets, but they were very hot and uncomfortable.

One day, my squadron commander came in and told me, "Carl, I've got new orders for you."

"Great, am I going to the 36th fighter wing in Bitburg, Germany?" I asked.

He answered, "No, you're going to Okinawa, Japan. You'll be leaving out of Hamilton AFB near San Francisco."

I was excited to be leaving for Japan, but also somewhat disappointed that I wasn't joining what I felt to be the best outfit in the USAF.

Earlier, while in Columbia, South Carolina, I had attended an officer's club dance where I met a beautiful young lady named Cindy. She was my first great romance. After dating for several months, we became "engaged to be engaged," but now I had just received orders transferring me to Okinawa for at least a year. On a date that evening, she promised she would wait for me until I came back stateside. Later, while I was flying combat missions in Korea, I received a "Dear John" letter from her saying she had met someone else, and they were going to be married. I was so sad and angry that I didn't marry until many years later.

After arriving at Hamilton AFB in California, several of us, who were bachelors and second lieutenants, decided we didn't want to stay at the bachelor officers' quarters (BOQ) on base, but instead went to San Francisco and booked a big suite of rooms at the Mark Hopkins Hotel.

Going to a nearby print shop, we had business-sized cards made up saying "Air Force fighter pilot's party at the Mark Hopkins Hotel in suite number xxx at 8:00 p.m. this evening" and handed them out to all the pretty girls we met on the street. From the start, we had some fun parties.

One afternoon, a fellow pilot, who was also an avid motorcycle enthusiast, was talking to a patrol officer on the street and told him we were going to Okinawa soon.

The policeman said, "We're getting new motorcycles in a few days and auctioning off all of the old ones, which are perfectly maintained. Why don't you guys come down to our motor pool and buy some and take them over there." He told us that he could arrange for them to be shipped to Okinawa with us.

A couple of days later, we went to the auction, and all of us bought motorcycles. For $250, I bought a pristine condition Harley Davidson "74" (its 74-cubic-inch displacement was equal to 1,212 cubic centimeters) with an overhead cam. The bike was fast and powerful and had that now-famous Harley growl.

Since our ship wasn't scheduled to arrive for approximately two weeks, we rode north and south from San Francisco on the renowned coastal highway, State Route 1, and really enjoyed seeing the beautiful beaches and scenery. My claim to fame (dubious as it may be) is that I was the leader of the first motorcycle gang in California. When the ship was ready for departure, we loaded our "bikes" between huge stacks of cargo boxes in the storage hold and took them with us to Okinawa.

Carl at Shaw AFB in 1948 with Classmates

OKINAWA

When we arrived on the island, I was disappointed to see the condition of the base—rusting ships floating in the bay and all-worn-out Quonset huts as our living quarters. At the time, Okinawa was known as the "Armpit of the Air Force." There were so many mosquitoes that we had to use nets over the beds to protect ourselves while we slept. Most of our flying was routine: learning the area around the base, practicing formation flying, shooting touch-and-go landings, intercepting unidentified aircraft and generally adding to the number of flying hours in jets.

Periodically, each of the pilots in our unit was assigned the duty of manning a mobile control tower, which basically was an orange and white checkered box with glass windows mounted on the bed of a two and one-half ton truck taken out to the runway to assist pilots in their takeoffs and landing approaches. As both parties were equipped with powerful

VHF (Very High Frequency) radios, we could communicate with the pilots as they took off and returned to the base.

One day, while I was manning the tower, an approaching F-80 made a spiraling descent and entered the traffic pattern unannounced on the radio. As he passed overhead, I could tell that there was no sound coming from the engine. Turning to my buddy, I said, "Hold down the fort while I go see what's going on with the aircraft that is on final approach."

Jumping in a jeep, which was parked outside, I drove to the end of the runway as the jet made a perfect landing and silently rolled to a stop. Pulling alongside the jet, I saw the pilot open the canopy and wave at me.

"Did you have an engine flameout in the traffic pattern?" I yelled.

"No, everything's fine. I just shut the engine down to simulate a flameout, which I thought was the normal landing procedure here," the pilot cheerily answered. He was a new Air Force captain who had recently begun flying jets, and his decision to shut the engine off was absolutely the wrong thing to do. The proper way to simulate a flameout while landing was to reduce power only to the idle position in case you needed to perform a "go around" and had to bring in full power to resume flying. There was water off both ends of the runway and only a very short overrun, so had he not made a perfect landing, he would've ended up in the water.

Every two or three months, a flight group of Navy F4U Corsairs would launch from the USS Boxer, a 27,100-ton Essex-class aircraft carrier that cruised around Okinawa from the Philippines and the Luzon Strait to the East China Sea to our west. After takeoff, to avoid radar detection, they would fly low level over the water and simulate an attack at our Air Force Base. The purpose of the exercise was to maintain our readiness for an unexpected enemy attack by unidentified aircraft.

First built in 1938, the Navy F4U Vought Corsair was designed around a big engine, the Pratt & Whitney "Double Wasp" eighteen-cylinder double radial capable of 2,250 horsepower. In straight and level flight, the airplane could reach speeds of 450 mph. The powerful engine also changed much of the airplane's design. The altered power plant needed a huge propeller. Thus, a 13' 4" diameter prop was fitted to the fighter. Then, the Corsair's fuselage had to be modified so it sat higher in the air to give the prop clearance; however, ordinary straight wings at that height would have required longer and weaker landing gear. So, the distinctive bent wings were developed to permit a shorter undercarriage and beefed up landing struts. Additionally, the intakes for the aircraft's turbo-supercharger, intercooler, and oil cooler were placed in slots on the leading edges of the wings. Air passing through those slots gave the aircraft a very distinctive high-pitched whistling sound, and during WWII, the Japanese gave the fighter the name Whistling Death.

One morning, I was assigned as the tower officer. Our squadron had two F-80s on standby alert at the end of the runway anticipating an impending sneak attack by the Navy Corsair pilots. I was standing on the observation platform encircling the tower holding a flare gun, called a Very pistol, loaded with a green flare. My job, if I got an alert from central group operations, was to fire the pistol up in the air to let the two F-80s know they were supposed to start their engines and intercept the unidentified enemy aircraft.

Somewhat bored because of the lack of any activity, I was fiddling with the Very pistol, pointing it up and testing the hair trigger. Instantly, the pistol went off and the green flare shot up into the air. As I watched appalled at what I'd done, I saw the two F-80s start their engines and immediately take off.

Not having the authority to launch the two aircraft without clearance from operations, I thought, "Well, this is going to ruin my Air Force career for sure." After a few minutes of standing there thinking my future had just gone down the drain, I suddenly heard a squadron of Navy Corsairs approaching the runway low level, and as they passed by the tower, I saw my two buddies in the F-80s "hot" on their tails simulating shooting them down.

The telephone in the tower rang, and I ran inside to answer it. The wing commander, a colonel, asked, "Carl, how did you do that?"

"Sir, I had a premonition they were coming in and fired the flare launching the two aircraft on alert," I quickly answered.

"Good job, Lieutenant. You did very well!" he enthusiastically told me.

In the span of about one minute I had gone from being a possible participant at my own court-martial to being a "hero."

After a year, our tour was finished. We were preparing to return to the United States on June 25, 1950, when the wing commander called us into a briefing room at headquarters and said, "If you guys leave now we're going to be really shorthanded, and it looks like our wing soon will be going to Korea. When we move to combat, you guys will all be back over here to fight in the Korean War, so you might as well volunteer to stay." Without exception, we all decided to stay.

That night we had a big party at the officer's club, and everyone agreed that whoever survived in combat would go back to the United States and visit the families of those who were lost. Out of the thirty-two pilots in my unit, twenty-two were killed, and three barely survived after being captured and held in North Korean POW camps where they were brutally tortured and starved!

After arriving home from the war, I spent thirty days on leave traveling around the United States visiting most of their families—the toughest job I ever had and very emotionally draining. Many of the families looked upon me as a surrogate son to replace their loved one who had been killed or captured. One family in Florida whose son was killed virtually adopted me, and we have stayed in touch since the Korean War. All their children call me Uncle Carl, and my daughter called my buddy's parents, Grandma and Grandpa.

Carl on His Motorcycle in Okinawa

Mobile Control Tower

How long must I see the battle flags
and hear the trumpets of war?
Jeremiah 4:21 NLT

THE KOREAN WAR

In a surprise attack on June 25, 1950, a lone American C-54 cargo plane parked at Seoul International Airport was set on fire by several strafing Yak-9 enemy airplanes. The Army of the People's Republic of Korea (North Korea) had just crossed the 38th Parallel and entered the territory of the Republic of Korea (South Korea). The Korean Conflict had officially begun.

The Korean Conflict was the first war in which jet aircraft played a principal role. Fighter airplanes, including the renowned P-51D "Mustang" and the F4U "Corsair," both piston-engine, propeller-driven, World War II vintage airplanes, relinquished their roles to a new generation of faster, jet-powered fighters. Initially, the F-80C "Shooting Star" and the F9F "Panther" jets overran North Korea's prop-driven air force made up primarily of older Soviet airplanes. However, the balance of air superiority soon shifted to the North Koreans with the arrival of the swept-wing Soviet-built MiG-15, one of the world's most advanced jet fighters.

The Chinese intervention in late October 1950, bolstered the Korean People's Air Force (KPAF) of North Korea with their own version of the MiG-15 as well.

The fast, heavily armed MiG outflew first-generation jets like the U.S. Air Force's F-80 and posed a real threat to B-29 Superfortress bombers that were escorted by American and North Atlantic Treaty Organization (NATO) fighters. Soviet Air Force pilots, flying surreptitious missions for North Korea, quickly learned the West's aerial combat techniques and successfully attacked and shot down many of the bombers.

Initially, it seemed the North Korean forces would obtain a rapid victory due to superiority in men, armored vehicles, and the sheer quantity of firepower. Such superiority also extended to the aerial element of warfare. However, once the United States committed its air power to the war, the North Korean Air Force was rapidly depleted. At the beginning of the war, the P-51D Mustangs and early jet fighters operated by the United States roamed the skies over North Korea virtually at will. By October 1950, the Soviet Union had agreed to provide to North Korea air squadrons equipped with high-performance MiG-15 fighters along with the trained crews to fly them. Simultaneously, the Kremlin agreed to supply the Chinese and North Koreans with their own MiG-15s, as well as training for their pilots.

In response to North Korea's deployment of jets, P-51D squadrons from the USAF converted to the Lockheed F-80C Shooting Star, Republic F-84E Thunderjet, and then to the North American F-86 Sabre jet fighters. The USAF gained air superiority in the Korean theater after the initial months of the war and maintained it for the duration of the conflict.

"MiG Alley" was a name given by American pilots to the northwestern portion of North Korea where the Yalu River empties into the Yellow Sea. During the Korean War, MiG Alley was the site of numerous dogfights between U.S. fighter pilots and their opponents from North Korea (including some unofficially flown by Soviet airmen) and the People's Republic of China.

Soviet aircraft were painted with North Korean or Chinese markings, and the pilots wore either North Korean uniforms or civilian clothes to disguise their origins. Soviet MiG-15 regiments were based on Chinese fields in Manchuria, where, according to existing United Nation rules of engagement, they could not be attacked.

Many Soviet aviation units underwent preliminary training at bases in their nearby Maritime Military District. Russian air defense troops also began to arrive along the Yalu River, setting up radar installations, ground control centers, searchlights, and large numbers of mobile antiaircraft guns to defend against American and NATO attacks on the Chinese airfields. American Air Force units were instructed not to cross the Yalu River, even in combat. Despite the restrictions, U.S. pilots frequently took advantage of the "hot pursuit" exception, flying over China to attack MiGs across the Yalu River. Later, hot pursuit became active MiG hunting over Manchuria, with U.S. pilots maintaining a universal code of silence about the patrols.

The Korean War also marked a major milestone not only for fixed-wing aircraft but for rotorcraft, featuring the first large-scale deployment of helicopters for search and rescue missions and medical evacuation (medevac)—extensively using the two-passenger Bell 47G model and the six-passenger

Sikorsky H-19 "Chickasaw." Both helped reduce fatal casualties by ferrying the wounded to newly formed Mobile Army Surgical Hospitals (MASH).[7]

My fighter wing was scheduled to move from Okinawa to Itazuke, Japan, in September 1950. Before we received our new orders to leave, I decided I wanted to fly in combat immediately. Taking a new F-80 Shooting Star airplane that I had just picked up in Misawa, Japan, I flew to Itazuke, Japan, where the 49th fighter group was located. Checking in at group operations, I told the commander that I wanted to fly combat missions with them. He said, "We don't have any extra aircraft for you to fly."

I cheerily and naively responded, "I brought my own." They refueled me, armed my jet and I began to fly combat missions with them.

After a few days, their wing commander, a colonel, arrived in a staff car and came up to me saying, "Lieutenant, are you assigned to us?"

Hesitatingly, I answered, "No, sir."

He said, "I received a call from your commander, who told me that you're up here flying combat missions with us. I want you to get back to Okinawa because you are all scheduled to come up to the war as a unit; not individually."

When I returned to my home unit, my wing commander called me into his office and chewed my butt out for what I'd done. Then he finally grinned and said, "Alright, son, since you're the only current combat pilot around here, get back to your unit and train those other pilots how to fly in combat."

Relieved that I wasn't going to get into trouble, I smartly saluted him and left.

We moved the unit to Itazuke, Japan, the fighter base with which I now was very familiar, and I began showing the other pilots what I'd learned while flying combat missions with the 49th. The airfield was originally built in 1944 by the Imperial Japanese army air force.

The closest USAF base to the Korean Peninsula, the 8th Fighter Wing stationed at Itazuke initially provided air cover for the evacuation of American personnel from Korea on June 26, the day after the North Korean communist invasion.

During the day, the North Koreans had numerous convoys out in the open, moving south along the dirt roads. We attacked them mercilessly with our 50-caliber machine guns and 5-inch rockets, which, incidentally, were not very accurate. On every mission, we received intense small arms ground fire from the enemy troops below and occasionally from the quad-fifties (four 50-caliber machine guns mounted together) located with them. Most of the time, we came back to base with multiple bullet holes in our F-80s. Unfortunately, several times, we came back missing a buddy who had been shot down and was killed or captured.

At the start of the war, we had three fighter wings flying off the same small Japanese runway with no radar available to help control all the flight departures and landings. After returning from combat missions, because of low ceilings and limited visibility, we frequently had to descend into heavy clouds with just one small radio beacon to guide us back to the base for landing.

Eventually, a Ground Control Approach (GCA) facility was built to help guide us to our final approach and landing by their expert ground personnel. GCA is the oldest air traffic technique used to fully implement radar to assist a landing airplane. The system is simple, direct, and worked well even with untrained pilots. It requires close communication between ground-based air traffic controllers and pilots in the approaching aircraft. Only one pilot and airplane are guided at a time.

The controllers monitor precision-approach radar systems to determine the precise course and altitude of the approaching aircraft. Then, they provide verbal instructions, by radio, to the pilots to guide them to a landing. The instructions include both descent rate (the glide path) and heading (the course) corrections necessary to follow the correct approach path.

By following controller commands to keep the landing aircraft on both glide path and approach centerline, a pilot will arrive precisely over the runway's touchdown zone. To land, pilots must have the runway or runway environment in sight before reaching the landing decision height, usually two hundred feet above the ground.[9]

Going to our combat area of operations (AO) from Itazuke, we flew on a heading of 330 degrees to Korea and attacked large groups of enemy soldiers, truck convoys, and dug in gun emplacements. Refueling and rearming at Taegu, South Korea, we would go out and hit the enemy again.

Taegu sits in a basin surrounded by low mountains and a series of smaller hills to the east. The Geumho River flows along the northern and eastern edges of the city, emptying into the Nakdong River west of the city. In the summer, the mountains forming the basin trap hot and humid air, creating stifling hot days. Similarly, in winter, cold air settles in the basin freezing everything.

Usually, we tried to make three sorties each day. After the third attack, we quickly climbed to 35,000 feet and flew back to Itazuki, our home base, because Taegu had no overnight parking. I participated in fifteen missions like that until the infamous Inchon Invasion when we moved the entire outfit, including all aircraft, to Kimpo to be closer to the fighting and to shorten our turnaround time for our attacks into North Korea.

On our return flight back to Japan, we regularly left Pusan, South Korea, with only ninety gallons of fuel on board to take us a hundred miles to Itazuki. We homed on a beacon at Brady AFB and then picked up the GCA controller to assist in our landing. Our landing weather minimums were a two-hundred-foot ceiling and a half-mile visibility, many times in heavy rain and fog. Frequently, we were on final approach with only twenty gallons of fuel—just enough to land and, hopefully, get into the parking area before the jet engine "flamed out" (quit).

After moving to Kimpo, Korea, we slept in two-man pup tents on the bare ground without heat because there wasn't permanent housing for us. Several weeks later, we received large, squad-sized tents that we set up on wooden pallets for the floor and placed sandbags around the sides for protection from enemy incoming mortar and rocket attacks. Living conditions were miserable because it was the coldest winter Korea had experienced in over one hundred years.

To stay warm, we had to wear all our clothes twenty-four hours a day. Making things worse, we also could not shower for several weeks at a time because of the lack of potable water and bathing facilities. Regardless of the person's military rank, soon everyone smelled pretty "rank." (Yes, pun intended!)

Kimpo played a major role during the Korean War, and the USAF designated the airfield as Kimpo Air Base. On June 27, the USAF began evacuating 748 U.S. diplomats, military dependents, and civilians by air transport from Kimpo and Suwon Airfield to Japan. On the afternoon of June 27th, five F-82 Twin Mustangs were escorting four C-54 Skymaster aircraft out of Kimpo when the C-54s were attacked by five enemy fighters.

In the subsequent dogfights, three North Korean LA-7 propeller-driven fighters were shot down with no loss of U.S. aircraft in the first air battle of the war. Later that day, four American F-80C's shot down four Russian-built Ilyushin-II propeller-driven airplanes over Kimpo in the USAF's first jet-aircraft victory.[10]

Each morning we were awakened at 0400 hours for a flight briefing and then took off in the dark to engage the enemy at first light. One morning, as a flight leader of four F-80's, I found a long enemy train parked in a tunnel with its engine sticking out one end and a few cars out the other. Seeing steam coming out of its smokestack, I immediately attacked the engine and blew it up.

Circling back around, we fired at the cars at the other end, not realizing the train was carrying ammunition. The massive explosion which occurred completely obliterated the tunnel and the mountain through which the tracks ran. The smoke and dust cloud rose to 30,000 feet and looked similar to the Hiroshima atomic bomb blast.

Later that night, as I faintly heard the familiar "putt-putt" sound of an airplane's radial engine, I thought to myself "Here comes Bed-Check Charlie" as he approached the Kimpo asphalt runway low level and dropped a fifty-pound bomb. The lone North Korean pilot attacked our base every night and dropped his only bomb on the runway to prevent our jets from taking off the next morning.

His aircraft was originally designed and built primarily in Russia, but during the Korean War, China was also involved in its manufacturing. Designated the AN-2, it was a highly versatile aircraft with a two-wing (biplane) configuration capable of extremely short takeoffs and landings. The AN-2 had a flight range of 525 miles and a top speed of 160 mph; however, the aircraft could fly as slow as thirty mph, allowing it to easily fly very close to the ground and under the U.S. radar facilities.

The next morning at the pilots' briefing, the wing briefing officer emphatically announced, "Do not take off on the right side of the runway! A deuce and a half truck is parked on that side, and a repair crew is filling in the crater hole caused by Bed-Check Charlie's bomb." The same warning was given to all the pilots at the group, squadron, and flight briefings.

After the morning briefing, our flight leader had gathered us all together before walking to the aircraft, and said, "We're going to line up in echelon formation (a group of aircraft flying in positions behind and to one side of the aircraft in front), with fifteen-second intervals between each takeoff. Number two, you'll slide over to the left. Number three, you'll already be on the left and number four, you'll need to slide over to the left behind number three. We need to do this to avoid hitting the repair crew and their truck."

Walking out to the flight line, a buddy of mine and I decided to switch aircraft. He ended up flying the number four aircraft, while I replaced him in number three. We didn't tell the flight leader of our decision to change airplanes because he was already strapping into his number one aircraft.

We all took off, following the leader, in fifteen-second intervals. As I passed by the truck, I remember thinking, "There's less than five feet clearance from my right wingtip to the back of the truck." Turning out of the take-off pattern, I saw my buddy in the number four aircraft behind me hit the truck and explode, causing a huge fireball as all the jet fuel, bombs, machine-gun ammunition, and rockets instantly ignited. He, along with the runway repair crew, was killed and the truck and aircraft were totally engulfed in flames.

Because I had switched planes with him, everybody thought I was in the number four aircraft and had died. A young airman, who worked in the large base operations tent, heard that I was killed. He was very superstitious, believed in ghosts and frequently had nightmares in which North Korean soldiers were sneaking up on him while he was asleep.

After our two and one-half hour attack mission was completed, we returned to Kimpo, were debriefed and I walked into the operations tent. The young airman saw me, screamed loudly and ran out of the tent, thinking he had seen a real ghost! He ran into a nearby Korean village and hid out for three days until his buddies finally found him and told him the truth—that I was alive.

The North Korea AO was a target-rich environment with lots of enemy ground troops, truck convoys, and equipment that we attacked with our fifty-caliber machine guns, five-hundred-pound bombs, and rockets. Many times, we flew out on reconnaissance missions looking for "targets of opportunity," which we could then destroy. Several months later, forward air controllers (FACS) were sent in flying slow T-6 single-engine airplanes, and they found many more targets for us to attack and destroy.

In the spring of 1951, American ground troops had very well-defined forward lines with trenches, foxholes, and gun emplacements set up facing to the north. Our primary flight missions were to attack the North Korean or Chinese ground troops that were moving south to oppose the American and NATO military forces. We flew in flight groups of four F-80 jets carrying armament consisting of six, fifty-caliber Browning M3 machine guns and forty-four hundred pounds of five-inch rockets, napalm, and bombs. Each of the machine guns was capable of firing three hundred rounds per minute; therefore, six could place eighteen hundred rounds per minute on a target.

I still vividly remember my first combat mission because we were bombing targets north of Taegu in a deep valley where the North Koreans had long slow-moving truck convoys on a dirt road. As I descended into the valley, the enemy troops began to fire their small arms at me and then several fifty-caliber machine gun positions located on the hilltops started shooting at me too.

The sun was beginning to set, and in the darkening skies, the brightly colored tracers looked like a solid wall of bullets through which I was flying. I remember thinking, "Man, I have to do this ninety-nine more times before it's over!"

One of the maintenance officer pilots at Misawa, Japan, came up with the idea of mounting an additional one-hundred-gallon extension to each wingtip fuel tank, thereby extending the F-80s' flight range and time over target (TOT). The fuel tanks had no baffles inside to prevent the fuel, which weighed six hundred and forty pounds, from sloshing and moving around while the jet was maneuvering during an attack. Several times, the extreme "G" forces were so great the external tank ripped loose, hitting the tail section and causing the aircraft to immediately tumble uncontrollably out of the sky—killing the pilots before they could bail out. Ultimately, the modification was scrapped because of safety concerns.

I encountered MiG-15's flying in from Manchuria on twelve of my missions. Once, while attacking them, I managed to hit two of the enemy aircraft with my fifty-caliber machine guns. Both began smoking badly but quickly descended into the clouds below to escape my relentless gunfire. I didn't see them hit the ground, and my gun camera was not working, so I was not given credit for the kills.

In late fall, a formidable group of North Korean and Chinese troops ambushed a much smaller column of U.S. Marines. In that attack, known as the Hwachon Reservoir Ambush, there were so many enemy soldiers swarming down the hill they seemed like ants boiling out of an anthill. I rolled in to attack them and expended my entire ordinance, as did all the other aircraft in my flight attack group. Along with U.S. Navy fighters, we stopped the enemy's advance and helped prevent a massacre of the Marines. Our much-needed assistance helped them escape.

Early one evening after completing one hundred combat missions, I was sitting in the officer's club tent when the wing commander came up and told me there were two C-54s landing at the base. He said, "Carl, I want you to go to the maintenance section, select fifty mechanics, and take them back to Itazuke (Japan) to form a rear echelon maintenance section."

"Sir, I don't know anything about maintenance," I said.

Turning to leave the tent, he replied over his shoulder, "Then, Captain, you better learn really fast!"

I had just made "spot" (temporary) captain, so I hurried down to the maintenance area, found my line chief and instructed him to round up fifty mechanics and other maintenance personnel and load them with all their clothing, gear, and tools on the two cargo planes to return to Itazuke, Japan.

We arrived at the Japanese base at 0100 hours. There was no one around base operations, but sitting outside was a deuce and a half truck with its engine idling. I furtively "commandeered" (military jargon for borrowed) the truck and loaded as many maintenance people as could fit and began to look for a place to stay. Arriving at the small housing area, I saw a group of empty tents with lights on. Unloading everyone, I sent the truck back to ferry the others to the tents where they were to bed down.

After everyone had been settled in, I had the driver take me to the BOQ where I told the clerk I needed a place to stay. I was absolutely worn out after flying combat missions for nine months, fulfilling the duties of the squadron adjutant, and now, serving as the only maintenance officer on the base. He assigned me to a room, and I fell onto the bed fully clothed and instantly went to sleep.

Early the next morning, an Air Force major began vigorously shaking my shoulder and angrily said, "Are you the captain that stole my unit's sleeping quarters last night? I've got a company of transport personnel coming in today, and those were my tents."

Yawning, I said, "All right, Major. I'll go find someplace else for my maintenance people to stay." I got up, found the line chief, and we found other quarters in which our maintenance troops could sleep that night.

The following morning, no airmen showed up for company formation because everyone had gone downtown to the geisha houses and spent the night carousing. Standing at the head of the non-existent formation, I turned to the master sergeant, who was a big burly guy and said, "Chief, what are we going to do about this?"

He said, "Captain, don't worry about it. I promise you everyone will be here tomorrow morning."

The next morning, everyone was shakily standing there in formation, although many had black eyes, bloodied noses and lips, scrapes, and bruises on their faces. The sergeant stood firmly at attention in front of the formation looking straight ahead stoically. His demeanor positively conveyed the message *Ask me no questions, and I'll tell you no lies.* So, I didn't.

A few days, later the wing commander called me from Korea saying, "Carl, I want you to perform the one-hundred-hour routine inspection on each of the aircraft, patch up any bullet holes and send them back to me after you perform a test flight." A few days after that, he called me again and said, "I'm going to start sending all of the new pilots to you first to check them out, and then you send them on to our unit."

Somewhat exasperated, I said, "Sir, there are no gunnery ranges here."

He responded by saying, "Find a deserted offshore island and use that as your target range." It was an unorthodox solution but worked.

At Itazuke, I was the only officer and pilot responsible for the whole rear echelon operation, including teaching the new pilots how to strafe and fire rockets. One morning, the maintenance chief came in and told me we didn't have enough tires for the unit's one T-33 training jet. He said, "I can remove the landing gear from an F-80 and install it in the T-33." I told him to go ahead and do that.

A few days later, a short, mustachioed full colonel from the Inspector General's (IG's) office in Tokyo walked in the operations building and came over to my desk. Glaring at me for a moment, he gruffly said, "Captain, only the Chief of Staff of the Air Force has the authority to make a modification like you've done to the T-33. I'm going to have you court-martialed."

Nonplussed, I said, "Colonel, if you don't like what I've done, you can call my wing commander in Korea and discuss it with him."

He called the wing commander on one of my field phones. My commander said, "If you don't like it, come up here and fly five combat missions with my wing and then we can discuss the issue." The IG colonel slammed the receiver down and without saying a word went back to Tokyo. We never heard from him again.

Later, my wing commander called and told me to change the landing gear back, and he would ship me enough tires so

I would have a sufficient supply of them in my warehouse for the T-33.

In addition to being the maintenance officer, I was responsible for paying all the personnel in my outfit. Once, when I flew up to Taegu to pay our troops, a friend of mine, Bob, who had finished his one hundred combat missions at the same time I did, came over to me and said, "Carl I think I'm going to fly a couple of more missions."

Shaking my head, I said, "You've been shot up as much as I have and I don't think that's a good idea."

He said, "Just two more missions, then I'll be done." On the second mission, when the flight group came back and landed, his plane was not with them.

We learned that he had been shot down and captured by the North Koreans. He spent two years in a POW camp and was very badly beaten by them. Frankly, I thought he had died in captivity. Several years later, I was at Nellis Air Force Base on the gunnery team and sitting in the operations building, when Bob tapped me on the shoulder and said, "Carl, if you have any more advice for me, I'll be glad to take it now."

Early one morning, shortly after the Inchon Invasion, two C-47s landed at Kimpo to ferry several pilots, including me, back to Itazuke to pick up more F-80s. I walked to the first aircraft, placed my boot on the lowest step of the ladder and started to climb in; then, for some unexplained reason, I decided to ride in the other cargo plane. Moving over, I climbed in and sat down. The plane I was in took off first and shortly after that, the second one did.

While flying over the Sea of Japan, the second airplane disappeared without a trace or any emergency radio calls and was never seen again or found. There was no debris field nor bodies recovered. The aircraft just disappeared into thin air. That was one of the many instances when the good Lord watched over me and saved my life.

One of the first pilots killed in Korea was Captain Tommy M. from my unit, whose wife had given birth to a baby girl several weeks earlier. He was shot down within the first two weeks we were operating out of Kimpo. Several pilots in his flight group flew down and circled low level over where he had bailed out, looking for him. After a short time, they saw several North Korean soldiers walking him down a dirt street in a nearby village with a rope around his neck and his hands tied behind his back. He was never heard from or seen again.

Note: Eleven years ago in 2006, I was on an Internet website that contained inquiries from family members looking for information about pilots who had died in the Korean War. I posted a message saying I had flown there in the early days of the war and might have information about some of the pilots who had been killed or were missing. An hour after I posted the message including my telephone number, a woman called from San Francisco and asked me if I had ever known Captain Tommy M., her father.

She got very excited when I told her I served with him in the same unit, and we flew together. She told me her mother had remarried one year after her father had been presumed killed in 1950, and never wanted to answer any questions about him.

She arranged to fly to Scottsdale, Arizona, where I lived, to learn more about her father and what he was like at the time he was shot down. I called two other friends who had also known him and let her talk with them too. She was very grateful to meet with us and said that after nearly fifty-six years, our meeting finally provided closure for her.

In my first year after returning from the Korean War, I met with several families of pilots with whom I had served and who had been killed in combat. Emotionally, the visits were very nerve-wracking and upsetting, but they were an obligation which I felt necessary for me to do.

In 1952, I received orders transferring me from Nellis Air Force Base to Pinecastle Air Force Base in Orlando, Florida, on a PCS. When I arrived in Orlando, I remembered my friend, Albert, whom I served with in Korea and Japan, was from Branford, Florida, and I still had his home address. I wrote to his family and offered to visit with them and talk about their son who had been killed. Within a few days, his mother called me and asked me to come spend the weekend with them at their home.

At the time, a buddy and I were renting a house located in what would later become Disney World. We had a wonderful weekend with my friend's family, and they entertained us for two days. They treated me like a member of the family, and I've stayed in close touch with them since.

Several months earlier while in Japan, after Albert and I had completed our one hundred combat missions, and we were awaiting orders returning us to the United States, he and I alternated conducting test flights for the F-80s that came out of routine maintenance work. At the time, we were flying out of the old Japanese kamikaze base of Tsuiki that had been reactivated as a U.S. Air Force Base and was hosting several fighter squadrons and maintenance facilities.

One day, an F-80 was ready for a test flight. As an additional duty, I had recently been designated as the squadron adjutant and had been assigned a desk job doing paperwork, so Albert said, "Why don't you let me take this one up?" I reluctantly agreed, and he went out to the airplane and took off. The tip tanks were supposed to be empty for all test flights, but for some reason this time, they had about a hundred gallons of JP-4 jet fuel in each of them, which weighed about 650 pounds.

Taking a stretch break from sitting so long at my desk, I walked outside and watched Albert take off and climb to approximately five thousand feet. When he made a tight, high "G" (gravity) turn, one of the partially filled tip tanks broke loose, striking his horizontal stabilizer. As I watched in horror, the jet immediately spiraled out of control and crashed into the Sea of Japan, instantly killing Albert

The water depth was two hundred fifty feet deep, and we didn't have any equipment or ability to recover the aircraft or his body. His mother was preparing to fly to San Francisco and await his return from the Korean War zone. Broken-hearted after being notified of his accidental death, she stayed in Florida and never stopped grieving his untimely loss. At the time, Albert was twenty-two years old, and I was twenty-three.

Shortly after the accident, new F-86s arrived in Korea, and I requested permission from the wing commander to let me fly another one hundred missions in the newly arrived jets. The North Koreans had Russians, who were poorly trained pilots, flying their MiG-15's, and I knew if I could attack them in the F-86s, I could shoot many of them down. The request was denied because I had been shot up so many times on my first hundred combat missions. Soon, my orders came in assigning me to Luke AFB, west of Phoenix.

The Korean War was over for me, and although I was happy to have survived, I was deeply saddened by the loss of so many of my friends and comrades. Even today, I remember what everyone looked like in their early twenties and still miss them. The old adage "time heals all wounds" is mistaken. Time has dulled the pain of my old emotional wounds created by the loss of so many of my pilot friends but has never healed them. Ask any combat veteran, and they'll agree with me.

1st DFC Korea

Korea F-80 Bomb Load

Korea F-80 Bomb Load

Korea Pup Tent Quarters

F-84 Armament

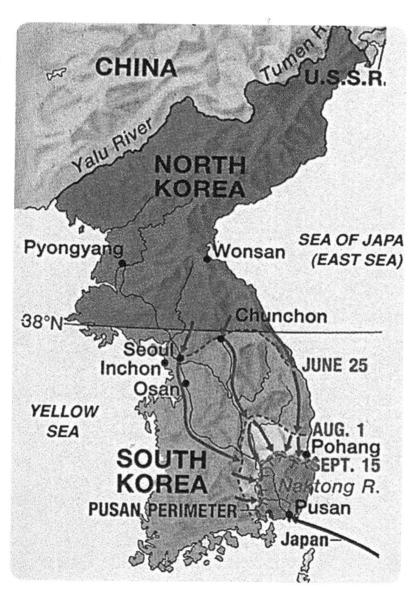

Korea War Map

Korean War F-80 Rearming .50 Caliber Machine Guns

HOME SWEET HOME

rriving at my new squadron at Luke AFB, I learned very quickly the pilots were very cliquish and treated new guys like lepers. After several days of sitting around and not being scheduled to fly, I was irritated because I was the only combat pilot who had returned from the Korean War.

One day, the wing commander came in for a briefing and said, "I need one pilot to volunteer to go to Nellis AFB to fly F-86s." Instantly, I raised my hand and volunteered. I went to the BOQ, packed my B-4 bag (a gray, soft-sided military suitcase) and immediately drove to Las Vegas.

Arriving at Nellis in mid-1951, I learned I was the first returning combat pilot in the squadron, and those guys treated me like I was royalty. Several months later, I received a call from a sergeant in my unit at Luke, and he said, "We've been looking for you, lieutenant (I had reverted back to my former rank when I left Korea). You've been AWOL for several weeks."

I replied, "I had to get to Nellis for my new assignment and thought you guys would be notified."

He replied, "Don't worry about it. I'll take care of everything." I never heard anything more about my sudden departure.

The new F-86s had not yet arrived, and we were flying the older F-80s; however, any time one of the new jets flew in, I would go sit in the cockpit with the Dash-1 (the aircraft operating manual) and memorize flight procedures and instrument locations. By doing that, I had about fifty hours of cockpit time before our new airplanes arrived.

Later, at a briefing for all of the pilots, the squadron commander announced we were now ready to transition from the F-80 jets to the new F-86s. He told us, "Major John R. is coming here soon, and he's got more F-86 time than anybody else in the U.S. Air Force. He's going to grill each one of you with a four hundred-question oral examination, and you better know your stuff. The first one of you to pass the exam will be the first one to fly the new aircraft."

Knowing I had nearly fifty hours learning the Dash-1 material, I volunteered to take the first exam. After correctly answering the first one hundred questions, Major R. said, "Carl, you know more about this airplane than I do, so you passed the exam, now go fly!"

I went out to the flight line with my helmet and parachute, climbed into the F-86, started it up and took off. Climbing to 35,000 feet, I leveled off and then pushed the nose over in a dive. Within a couple of seconds, I watched the Mach meter needle go past "1", indicating that I had broken the sound barrier for my very first time.

I needed to grasp the stick with both hands because the early model jets would roll to the left if you didn't. But even with that, going faster than the speed of sound was exhilarating for me, and I realized during that flight, the personal thrill of fulfilling my long ago wish made to that crusty recruiting sergeant of becoming a jet fighter pilot.

After flying the F-86 for about an hour, I returned to Nellis, landed and walked into squadron operations. "How did it go?" my commanding officer asked.

I answered, "Okay, sir, no problems at all."

He said, "All right, then. We will put you on the schedule now."

I started flying gunnery training sorties and volunteering for test flights, so I was averaging about seventy-five flight hours per month. On the weekends, because I was a bachelor, I would check out an F-86 and fly cross country around the United States from Maine to San Francisco to log the required night and weather experience that we couldn't get in Las Vegas.

One day, I was getting ready to take off on a mission when a colonel came up to me and said, "Carl we're getting ready to set up a gunnery school at Pinecastle Air Force Base (later renamed McCoy AFB). If you'll go down there and help me set it up, I'll make you a flight commander."

So, I thought, "What the heck," and quickly replied, "Yes, sir, I'll go."

Before I left Nevada, however, a hilarious event occurred. Captain "Nifty" (Mac) McCrystal always seemed to be involved in mischief, pranks, and unusual situations. Since we were encouraged to fly aircraft on cross countries to gain experience in night flying in inclement weather, he checked out a T-33 one Friday afternoon at Nellis AFB to fly to San Antonio's Kelly AFB to see his sister and her family and then fly on to Riverside, California. When he arrived in San Antonio, his sister and family met him at the airfield.

While he was greeting the family, his sister said, "Mac, I see that you have an empty backseat. I have a large glass fishbowl that I would like to send to our sister in Riverside. Do you think you could carry it in the backseat with you because I'm afraid it will be broken if I try to ship it?"

"Sure, Sis, I can do that," he cheerily answered.

After visiting with his family, he took off at midnight on Saturday night, intending to fly to Davis-Monthan AFB in Tucson and refuel; however, there was a very strong jet stream flowing from the west that slowed him down. Arriving over El Paso, Texas, he saw he was running low on fuel and decided to land at Biggs AFB—a highly secretive and heavily guarded Strategic Air Command Base (SAC) containing a large supply of nuclear weapons and long-range bombers.

Instead of radioing his flight-following controller and changing his flight plan to include refueling at Biggs, which would've been a routine procedure, he turned off all his exterior lights at thirty thousand feet and began a high rate of descent by performing a "Split S" aerobatic maneuver— intending to land at the base unannounced.

Buzzing the tower, low level, he entered the empty traffic pattern and quickly landed on the main runway. Of course, prior to touching down, he had been picked up on radar as an unidentified and unresponsive hostile aircraft. The base commander was immediately notified, and an emergency alert was issued requiring all available military police to proceed to the end of the runway in their vehicles with weapons drawn and lights flashing.

Touching down on the runway, Mac saw the line of security police vehicles at the other end. Instead of taxiing up to them and stopping, he swiftly exited the runway and taxied to base operations. Arriving there, he hurriedly shut the engine down, set the brakes, opened the canopy and climbed out after removing his flight helmet. Unstrapping the fishbowl in the rear seat, Mac climbed back in the front seat and put it over his head.

A huge MP driving a jeep screeched to a halt next to the T-33 and jumped out with his .45 pistol drawn. He shined a big bright flashlight into Mac's monstrously magnified face. Mac then announced, "I'm from another planet. Many more of my kind will follow me. Take me to your leader!"

Mac was taken into base operations at gun point where the wing commander and several colonels awaited his presence. He tried to explain who he was and where he had come from, but he had forgotten his wallet at his sister's house with all his identification.

The wing commander at Biggs called the wing commander at Nellis and asked, "Do you have a Captain McCrystal in your unit?"

"Oh, God! What has he done now?" the Nellis commander asked. After a brief conversation, the Nellis commander asked to speak to Mac telling him, "Get your butt back here immediately!"

The Biggs commander told Mac, "Captain, don't you ever come back to this base!"

F-80 Nellis AFB

F-86 Nellis AFB

PINECASTLE AIR FORCE BASE

L eaving Las Vegas, thirteen other combat veterans and I formed a convoy of cars and partied all the way to Orlando, Florida. After checking into the only building on the base, the new wing commander received us and said, "What are you guys doing here now? We don't have any quarters for you, and the runways are not finished. For the next thirty days, you won't have anything to do, and this will probably be the only times in your careers that you'll have a "boondoggle." I want everyone to stay together and every two to three days check in with me so that I will know where you're located."

As we went back to the motel, our commanding officer, who was a major, told everyone, "All right, guys. The colonel says we don't have to do anything for thirty days, but we are a military organization, so we are going to have a mandatory, daily staff meeting at 1700 hours in my room." I saw several pilots murmuring under their breath while looking at each other. Then, continuing, he said smiling, "I don't want to see anyone show up who doesn't have a cold six pack of beer!"

We partied for the next thirty days driving to Daytona Beach, Miami, Key West, and Tampa. Finally, the wing commander called to tell us the base was finished. We had to come back and go to California to begin picking up F-80s and T-33s to train the combat pilots going to Korea.

We ran the gunnery school for about a year. Then one day, a brigadier general landed in a B-47 turbojet-powered, swept-wing strategic bomber, looking for fighter pilots who wanted to transition into the multiengine aircraft. Many of the old B-24 and B-29 pilots were having trouble with the new jet-powered bombers, so he was looking for fighter pilots to begin multiengine jet training. I politely declined the training and continued to stay at Pinecastle. I had no interest in leaving fighter jets to fly bombers.

One morning, my roommate came to me and said that he was going to marry a girl in St. Louis; however, he had just received orders for Laughlin AFB in Del Rio Texas, which had no base housing. He asked me if I would go in his place. At the time, I was dating a girl off and on in San Antonio and decided to go to Del Rio in his place so I could be closer to her.

When I arrived at Laughlin AFB in Del Rio, I was disappointed to see most of the buildings were old World War II wooden structures that were very rundown and in need of repair and paint. The base operations building was just as dilapidated as everything else.

A year earlier, before arriving in Orlando, I was promoted to permanent captain. I had spent a lot of time scheduling pilots at Luke, Nellis, and Pinecastle and was a hard worker, so at Laughlin, I was given an office located over the base operations building and ended up in a lieutenant colonel's job as the assistant group operations officer handling all the scheduling of the pilots and aircraft. My office had big glass windows overlooking the airfield so I could see the planes taking off, flying in and landing.

On several occasions, an Air Force Major General arrived in his customized "VIP" B-17 bomber and taxied up to the operations building visitors' parking ramp. He flew in unannounced to check on our wing commander, who was not doing a very good job.

One Sunday morning at 0800 hours, his plane entered the traffic pattern, landed and taxied up to base operations to park. I ran out to greet him. When he stepped out of the aircraft, I stood at attention and saluted. He looked at my name tag and said, "Schneider, every time I come in, it looks like you're the only guy who ever works around here. Why aren't you a major?"

I answered, "Sir, it wouldn't hurt my feelings."

He pointed his finger at me and said, "You'll be on the next promotion list for major that comes out." The combination of my hard work and the Major General's keen attention to the men under his command led to me becoming a major four years ahead of my classmates.

Several times while stationed at Laughlin, we drove to Ciudad Acuna, across from Del Rio in Old Mexico, to eat at a delightful Mexican restaurant called "Ma Crosby's." They served the tastiest margaritas and fantastic Mexican food. Very famous, the restaurant has been mentioned in several country-western songs by George Strait, Willie Nelson, and others. Unfortunately, Ma Crosby's closed in 2011, after the drug cartels and narcotics traffickers made going into Ciudad Acuna too dangerous for *Norte Americanos.*

As my girlfriend lived a hundred fifty miles away in San Antonio, I frequently would finish flying early, get in my Cadillac, let the "hammer down," and pick her up for dinner and a movie. After taking her home, I returned to the base in time to catch four or five hours of sleep before I had to fly again. Ah! Youthful, exuberance, and stamina.

I spent two and a half years at Laughlin. Then, one day I flew to Luke AFB to try out for the Air Force Thunderbirds' precision-flying team. Their commander had me fly the right wing in a demonstration flight and afterward came up and said, "Okay, Carl you're going to be the new right wingman. Go back to Texas, and I'll have the orders cut assigning you to the team."

When I got back to Laughlin, I walked into the officer's club and saw the wing commander, who was coming out. Saluting him, I excitedly said, "Colonel, I'm going to Luke AFB to fly with the Thunderbirds."

Smiling, he said, "No, you're not, Carl. An hour before your orders came in for the Thunderbirds, other orders came in sending you to the Marine Corps on an exchange assignment." I was disappointed about the change of assignments but determined to make the best of it.

PINECASTLE AIR FORCE BASE

Before reporting to the Marines in Quantico, Virginia, in 1954, I was sent on a temporary duty assignment (TDY) to Nellis AFB to attend the F-86 fighter weapons school for six weeks. After the training, I returned to Laughlin Air Force Base and started getting ready for the move to Virginia.

Then, I learned my unit was going to be given a trophy for having zero accidents or training incidents in two and half years of flying. The President of the United States, along with the Chairman of the Joint Chief of Staff, the Secretary of the Air Force, and many other congressmen and dignitaries came to Laughlin AFB for the presentation of the trophy.

Everyone was sitting in the VIP sections of a grandstand bleacher temporarily set up next to the runway, and I arranged a flyover of forty-eight fighter aircraft of different types. I was leading the flight, and after we had made several low-level passes in front of the VIP seating, I made a long downwind leg and turned and set us up to land.

Forty-seven jet fighters landed perfectly, but the pilot flying the last one, number forty-eight, was so nervous that he touched down on the runway with his landing gear retracted (up), and sparks began flying all over the place. He slid to a spectacular stop perfectly, in front of all the VIPs. Needless to say, that ended his Air Force career. After some debate, our unit still received the big trophy because the pilot who had the accident was not assigned to our base.

This incredible story took on a life of its own. Once I retired from the Air Force, I was consulting with a company in Arizona, and the owner asked me to go on a road trip to the little town where he had been born so he could listen to more of my "war stories." As we were driving along, I told him the story about the "gear up" mishap in Del Rio. When I looked over at him, he wasn't smiling. I asked, "What's wrong?"

He answered by saying, "Let me tell you the rest of the story. Many years later, that pilot became my father-in-law, and I've heard the story numerous times."

He said that when his father-in-law came to a sliding stop in front of the VIP bleachers with sparks flying everywhere, he was tempted to pull the ejection-seat handle and shoot out through the canopy in front of the spectators as a grand finale "crowd pleaser." Fortunately, he didn't go through with that crazy plan and shortly after that, he left the Air Force."

Pinecastle AFB

FAMILY MATTERS

While TDY at Nellis AFB, I met my future wife, Elaine. I was casually dating a Las Vegas showgirl who kept telling me about this really "knockout" beautiful, blue-eyed blonde who was her roommate. On two occasions, I ventured over to their apartment, but the showgirl was on a date. The first time I went there, I asked Elaine if she would like to go out with me. Her reply to me was, "No way, buster, you're a bird-dogger— always chasing girls and never staying with one for long." About a week later, I went back to their apartment, and Elaine agreed to go out with me for a cup of coffee. We hit it off well, and in three months we were married.

Before we married, I said, "Elaine, here's the deal. I'm going to stay in the Air Force and fly every aircraft I can get my hands on, and it's a dangerous profession. We are going to move around a lot whenever a new airplane comes out, or I'm offered a new job." Continuing with my prepared speech, I said, "If we have children, you'll have to primarily raise them plus your own son, Bob, because I'm going to be away a lot. If there's another war, I'll be in it for sure. Also, if I am promoted to senior rank, we will have a lot of social obligations, and you'll have to handle that too. If you want to do all that, then let's get married. What do you say?"

Tearfully looking at me, she replied, "Sounds good to me, Carl. Let's do it." That was my proposal to her, she accepted, and we were married for forty-four wonderful years until she died in 1999.

Elaine was a model Air Force wife. She had worked hard while growing up on a farm in Nebraska and then taught school in Nevada after attending the University of Nebraska. She was a fine cook and a real charmer. When I made brigadier general several years later, my boss came up to us at a party and said, "Carl, you would not have made brigadier general without her." I heartily agreed!

I'd been a bachelor for a long time and was ready to settle down and have a family. After we had married, she remained in Las Vegas teaching school and finishing the spring semester while I returned to Del Rio. After school was out, she joined me at Laughlin AFB.

There wasn't any available base housing, so we stayed in other families' houses when they were away. Elaine loved Del Rio and Southwest Texas. She was a young widow whose husband had died when her son Bob was two years old. When we married, Bob was seven years old and lived with his grandmother in California until shortly before we left Laughlin.

Elaine quickly adapted to the Air Force lifestyle and the constant moving from one base to another. Because of her years of teaching school, she was very organized and could quickly and efficiently pack all our belongings when I was assigned to a new job requiring yet another move.

In those days, the Air Force frequently moved families every year with little regard to the hardship created for the wives and the children. Later, that policy changed to allow for more time between PCS moves which increased the retention rate for officers and enlisted personnel. The endless moving every year was especially hard on Bob who had never been exposed to new schools and locations prior to our marriage. Several years later, while I was stationed at MacDill Air Force Base, Bob came down to Tampa and joined the Air Force and served in Vietnam as a military policeman.

When we moved to Korea in 1971, Elaine was the only Air Force general's wife there, so whenever Air Force officials visited, she was responsible for supervising and entertaining their wives. This usually involved shopping trips to Seoul and organizing social events at the officers' club. Also, because we were officially approved with all the foreign embassies in the country, she and I were required to attend their parties two or three times per week. She was a trooper and never complained about our sometimes hectic and grueling social life.

Our daughter, Debi, who was born while I was stationed at Bitburg, Germany, was a delightful child—always making straight A's in school while growing up. Once, while she was a senior in high school in Korea, she came to Elaine and me and said one of her teachers wanted the students to write a story about an "adventure" they had experienced. Believing that she had not done much in the way of adventurous living, she announced she was going to take a trip to the eastern coast of Korea and spend a week living in a monastery with a group of monks, eating very little food and sleeping on the floor.

The teacher had arranged trips for other students previously and thought Debi would enjoy the unusual experience. Since Debi did not speak Korean, the teacher made up several flash cards in the Korean language which she could show to the indigenous population to communicate with them in that way. She spent a week sleeping on the hard kitchen floor along with a female cook and her two daughters. When she arrived back in Seoul, she greeted us, but never revealed any of the experiences she had while staying at the monastery!

Being dependents of an Air Force officer who moved as frequently as we did put an additional emotional strain on Elaine, Bob, and Debi. But, the moves also made them more resilient and adaptable to changing environments than a typical civilian family. Moving from airbase to airbase caused us to bond as a family as we relied on each other for mutual support.

Carl with Family and MG Holland

Elaine

MARINE CORPS TRAINING

As I walked into the headquarters building at Quantico, Virginia, a three-star Marine Lieutenant General was coming down the steps. I had just returned from a weeklong field training exercise (FTX) and was taking my son, Bob, with me to pick up some study materials for the Marine amphibious course in which I was enrolled. While out in the "boonies," I had not showered or cleaned up in over a week. I saluted the general as he walked up to me and stopped to tousle Bob's hair. "Son, when you grow up, are you going to be like your daddy?" he asked.

Bob promptly answered, "No, sir! I don't want to crawl around in the mud like he has been doing." The Marine general frowned and quickly walked away.

Two Air Force buddies of mine had been assigned to the same Quantico school. When we checked in, the first thing the instructors did was give us an entrance exam about all the terminology and jargon used in the Marine Corps. I had just made major, and my other two classmates were captains. Of all the students in the course, and to our chagrin, we made the lowest score on the examination because we didn't know anything about the Marines.

Later that evening, the three of us got together and decided to do whatever it took to graduate in the top ten percent of the class. We studied our butts off throughout the course, and we accomplished our goal. Once again hard work paid off for me.

Our Marine training was called the Amphibious Warfare School and was considered Junior training. After flying in combat, we resented being called Juniors. (Now it's referred to as the Marine Command and Staff College.) For three months, we ran with packs on our backs, fired various weapons, dug foxholes and trained just like any Marine "grunt."

The second phase of the course taught us how to coordinate air-to-ground operations and call in air support primarily. The third phase included training about amphibious assaults and the loading of the boats to land on shorelines. Several times, we trained on nearby Virginia beaches.

Air Force General Curtis LeMay visited Quantico to speak at one of the class functions, and afterward, the Marines had a reception for him at the officers' club. Since we were also in the Air Force, we were invited to the festivities. In the reception line, a three-star Marine general was standing next to four-star General Curtis LeMay.

As we approached General LeMay, he turned to the Marine general and asked, "What are you teaching my boys here?"

The Marine Lieutenant General said, "We are teaching them how to load boats."

General LeMay rolled the big cigar he was smoking, thought for a minute and then said, "Well, I guess boats are okay if you want to go fishing." It took all our powers of self-control not to burst out laughing.

Soon after graduating from the Marine course, a colonel in the Pentagon called me and asked, "Major what do you want to do now?"

I answered, "Sir, if you look in my personnel file you'll find numerous requests to be transferred to the 36th Fighter Group in Bitburg, Germany."

He replied, "Okay, anything else you want?"

"Yes, sir. I want to go to Nellis and get checked out in the F-100."

A few days later, I was transferred there; however, I wasn't put on the schedule to fly the F-100. After several days, I went to the scheduling officer and discovered he thought I had only been flying propeller-driven Marine SNJ-5 Texans, which were the same as the primary Air Force AT-6 training plane.

I pulled out my Form-5 (military flight time log) and showed him that I had flown F-80s, F-84s, F-86s and had been an instructor pilot at Nellis. I had more jet pilot flying time than anyone else there, so he said, "Go, ahead and start flying."

Without any instruction, that afternoon I went to the flight line, pre-flighted the aircraft, started the F-100, taxied to the end of the runway and, after getting clearance from the tower, took off. I became fully qualified in the supersonic fighter before moving to Germany.

Marine Emblem

BITBURG, GERMANY

Under contract with the United States, the French Army began construction of what became Bitburg Air Base in Western Germany's Eifel Mountains in the Rhineland-Pfalz in early 1951. Bitburg Air Base was officially established as a United States Air Forces Europe (USAFE) installation on September 1, 1952, after the arrival of the 53rd Fighter-Day Squadron, 36th Fighter-Day Wing. The wing converted to a nuclear-qualified fighter-bomber mission in 1958.

The remainder of the wing, the 22nd and 23rd Fighter-Bomber Squadrons, arrived with their F-84E Thunderjets in November 1952. The 36th was established as the 36th Fighter Wing on 17 Jun 1948. Ultimately, the 36th became the longest continuously based USAF unit in Germany having been stationed at Bitburg Air Base for forty-two years without interruption. The wing was deactivated on 1 Oct 1994, and the base was turned over to German authorities.

After six weeks' temporary duty (TDY) at Nellis, I received orders for Germany and was finally on the way to join my favorite fighter unit. My wife, Elaine, who was six months pregnant with Debi, returned to her hometown of Omaha, Nebraska, and moved in with her mother.

After a few weeks, Elaine moved into a small apartment in Omaha with Bob, whom I later adopted. He had contracted measles; my sister-in-law began taking care of him so that he was not around Elaine while he had the disease. When our daughter, Debi, had been born and was about six weeks old, I returned to the U.S. and took Elaine, Bob, and the baby to Texas to show off my family. After a week of visiting, we boarded a flight to New York City and then flew to Frankfurt, Germany, where we were met by a sponsoring family, who drove us to Bitburg. All of us had come down with the flu, so for about a week after we arrived, we were very sick; but, we had hired a full-time German maid, and she took very good care of us.

Before returning stateside to retrieve my family, I was chosen to be the chief gunnery officer because I'd graduated from the Fighter Weapons School at Nellis AFB. At the time, I was living in the BOQ. The fighter group operations facility was located nearby in a dimly lit underground building with charts and flight schedules covered with Plexiglas on the walls.

One night at the BOQ, I began to experience excruciating pain in my left eye. A friend of mine took me to the hospital where we were met by an ophthalmologist who examined my eye. The doctor said, "Major, we will be lucky if we can save your eye; but if we do, you'll never fly again!"

Very despondent and greatly concerned, thinking that my flying career was over, I stayed in isolation at the BOQ for thirty days, during which time the doctor periodically came to examine my eye. Finally, one day, after an examination, he said, "Carl, I've been an ophthalmologist for twenty-seven years, and I've never seen anybody recover from this ailment like you have." He cleared me to go back to work; however, I had to wear a black patch over my eye temporarily. After that emotional experience, I had 20/20 vision again.

After I had returned to my job, the group commander came into my office one day and said, "Carl, we've had three squadrons flying at the gunnery ranges in France. The weather's been so bad that one of them has not been able to fly very much and the other one had a lot of maintenance problems, so they haven't completed the training. The third one did a fantastic job because the weather was clear the entire time they were down there. The wing commander has decided to give the third squadron a trophy for doing so well. If he does that, it's going to severely hurt the morale of the entire unit, because it's not fair. As the chief gunnery officer, will you go talk to him and try to convince him not to give them the trophy?"

Somewhat puzzled by the request, I answered, "Yes, sir. I will."

The next day, I arranged a five-minute meeting with the wing commander—a full colonel. I walked into his office, stood in front of his desk with my black patch over my left eye, and held a salute as he continued working on something and didn't look up or return my salute.

I stood there for five minutes, occasionally quietly clearing my throat to get his attention. Finally, he looked up, saluted and gruffly said, "What do you want, Clark Gable?" He had taken acting lessons and could get very dramatic. He said, "Sit down, major." Then he swiveled his chair around with its back to me.

After a few minutes of just sitting there, he turned around, and his entire personality had changed. He asked me how my family was doing, where I was from, what sports I liked, how long I'd been in the Air Force, etc. We talked for forty-five minutes while several lieutenant colonels and colonels from my unit waited outside to learn if the trophy was going to be presented.

Finally, slyly looking at me, the colonel said, "You came in here to ask me not to present the trophy, didn't you?"

I answered, "Yes, sir. I did. It will be extremely bad for morale and a mistake if you do."

He replied. "All right, then I won't."

I jumped up, saluted him and said, "Thank you, sir." as I quickly walked out of his office before he could change his mind. Everyone in the outer office rushed up to me asking me what his decision was going to be. I told them there wasn't going to be any trophy presented. I was a big hero in the wing after that.

After a year as the chief gunnery officer, the wing commander called me into his office and said, "Carl, I want you to take the group maintenance officer in a T-33 and fly down to Wheelus AFB in Tripoli, Libya, and set up a gunnery school there".

Standing up, I saluted and said, "Yes, sir." and left his office.

Originally built by the Italian Air Force in 1923, Wheelus Air Base was located in the Kingdom of Libya. At one point, it was the largest U.S. military facility outside the United States with an area of twenty square miles on the coastline off Tripoli. The base had its own beach club, the largest military hospital outside the U.S., a multiplex cinema, a bowling alley, and a high school for five hundred students. The base also had its own radio and TV station as well as a shopping mall and fast food chain outlets. At its height, Wheelus had over 15,000 military personnel and their dependents on base. The U.S. Ambassador to Libya once called it "a Little America on the sparkling shores of the Mediterranean," although temperatures at the base frequently reached 110 to 120 degrees Fahrenheit.

In February 1958, the 20th Fighter-Bomber Wing in England established an operational detachment at Wheelus AFB. This detachment managed the USAFE Weapons Training Center for month-long squadron rotations by the European fighter wings.

USAFE units from Germany, such as the 36th and 20th Tactical-Fighter Wings participated in gunnery operations with their F-84 Thunderjets and the F-100 Super Sabres. They trained in air-to-air and air-to-ground gunnery, and delivery of conventional ordinance and nuclear "shapes" at the weapons range about ten miles east of the air base.

After filing a flight plan, I walked to my plane, climbed into the front seat, and we took off from Bitburg. After we had begun our flight en route to North Africa, our radios went out, so I landed at a French Air Force base in Marseille, France, to see if they had a radio-repair shop. Nobody was around except a refueling crew because it was late afternoon on a Friday, so I got on one of their tall ladders, opened the avionics inspection port on the side of T-33 and kicked the radio console with my boot. Turning the aircraft ignition on, I checked the radios, and they worked fine.

As we crossed over Sicily, towering thunderstorms appeared reaching 40,000 feet and stretching from Tunisia to Egypt. The cloud tops were sheared off by the Jetstream and were called "anvil top" because they were flat, looking like a blacksmith's anvil. We had a British air traffic controller who was handling our flight following en route, so I called him on the radio and asked for a weather report at the Wheelus Air Force Base in Tripoli. In his most proper British accent, he said, "I say, governor; it's a six hundred feet ceiling and one-half-mile visibility with heavy rain."

I responded by asking, "What do you think we should do?"

He laughingly answered, "Well, governor, you can bail out now or bail out later; it's up to you."

Continuing to Wheelus, I descended IFR (on instruments) down into the dark clouds. When I broke out of the overcast, I was neatly lined up with the runway, but could just barely see it because of the heavy rain. We touched down and taxied to base operations, but had to wait an hour for the heavy rain and wind to stop blowing before opening the canopy.

The runway had recently been worked on, and there was a vertical three-foot drop-off at the approach end where I had just landed. If I had touched down short, the copilot sitting in the backseat and I would have crashed and burned—another example where the Hand of Providence saved my life.

F-100 at Bitburg

F-100 Super Sabre at Bitburg

BUZZ ALDRIN

Buzz Aldrin and I were F-86 instructor pilots at Nellis Air Force Base in the early 1950s when we received orders assigning us to Bitburg, Germany. We were both assigned to the 22nd Fighter Squadron—I was a major, and he was a captain. I had four flights under my command, and he was my "A" flight commander. Any special missions that I had, or problems needing to be solved, I gave to Buzz because he was extremely analytical, detailed, smart and a fantastic pilot.

Several times on Fridays, when we were sent to Wheelus AFB gunnery training in North Africa, we had the mess sergeant cook fried chicken for us. We took our sleeping bags, ice chests, facemasks, and spear guns to the nearby Mediterranean beach and explored the underwater Roman ruins. Cartographers from a United States geological survey team were there as well. We slept on the beach at night and had a thrilling time snorkeling, shooting fish, and swimming in the crystal-clear blue water.

One night in 1957, it was very clear. We could see millions of stars overhead because there was no ambient light from any nearby towns or villages. Earlier in the day, we had been told the Russians had just launched an orbiting satellite called "Sputnik."

While we were lying on the beach, we saw the satellite cross the starry sky looking like a slow-moving comet. Turning to Buzz, I said, "You know, someday someone is going to fly in space, and they're going to be called astronauts. You ought to be one of those guys." He didn't respond, and we didn't discuss it any further. But, I've always wondered about his thoughts at that moment and if he had any idea of his future and the impact he would have on our nation's space program.

Returning to Tripoli on Sunday after our spearfishing exploits, we took the fish to the chef at the Underwater Explorers Club where we were members. The chef prepared a fabulous tray of seafood, garnished with an assortment of delicious vegetables. All the pilots had navy blue blazers with gray slacks and matching red ties that we wore to all semi-formal occasions. Life was good for us as we sat around a big table overlooking the beautiful Mediterranean Sea, eating freshly caught fish and drinking beer. Those were very memorable times for all of us—flying F-100 Super Sabres, firing our machine guns on the desert gunnery range during the day and shooting fish with our spear guns under water on the weekends.

Buzz and his wife lived in the apartment next door to ours, so we frequently got together after work to visit and chat. Since I was his rating officer, I wrote his officer's effectiveness report (OER) and recommended (as he had requested) that he be sent to MIT to study astronautics and earn his Doctorate of Science (ScD), which he did upon returning from Germany.

Although he never was a test pilot, he was given orders ultimately to enter the third astronaut training class in October 1963. Many times, he worked out docking problems in space and the NASA engineers deferred to his calculations and recommendations. Then, on July 20, 1969, Buzz and Neil Armstrong landed the Apollo 11 capsule on the moon and were the first humans to set foot on its surface—probably the greatest "test" of his aeronautical piloting skill and courage.

As an American and a friend of his, I was enormously proud of Buzz when he landed on the moon, knowing I had played a very small part in this historic achievement.

Astronaut Buzz Aldrin

E&E TRAINING

Periodically, the fighter squadrons in Europe were brought in for several days to learn how to escape from and evade the Russians and the Warsaw Pact (War Pac) countries in the event we were shot down while delivering nuclear weapons on a target if World War III began. War Pac was a defense treaty among the Soviet Union and seven of its Soviet satellite countries in Central and Eastern Europe. During the Cold War, their treaty was created after West Germany was admitted into the NATO.

After the classroom instruction, we all loaded into two and one-half ton trucks (called a deuce and a half) and were taken out into the night and dropped off in the middle of a large forested area covering several hundred square miles. My E&E partner thought he knew where we were located and insisted we go north. After a brief discussion, I finally agreed. A U.S. Army brigade and several participating French units were selected as the opposing force "bad guys" to search for us. Whoever found a downed pilot would be rewarded with a weekend pass. Additionally, the local German police had been notified of the training exercise and were offered a fifty-dollar reward for each one of us they found. All our enemy opposition were highly motivated to locate and take us into custody.

If they captured us, then we were going to be transported to an old castle in Trier, Germany, where they would strip us down to our shorts and put us in cold, empty rooms without bedding or blankets and feed us bread and water for three days. So, we were just as highly motivated to avoid capture as they were to capture us.

When the sun came up the next morning, we realized we had been traveling in the wrong direction and turned around and headed the other way. By the time we got to the "enemy" lines, where the French and U.S. Army troops had been posted to look for us, they were gone. We hid in a heavily forested area about ten acres in size under an outcropping of branches, leaves, and brush. After a while, we spread out our orange signaling panel, hoping a friendly helicopter would see it and rescue us.

Early the following morning, a dog started barking excitedly from a nearby farm house that had some sheep pens full of lambs. The barking alerted the opposing force bad guys that something was wrong and they began to search for us intensely. There was a clearing nearby just big enough for a helicopter to land. In a few minutes, a chopper flew overhead, saw our signaling panel, quickly made an 180-degree turn and landed with its doors open. Like a couple of scared rabbits, we started running and dove headfirst into the helicopter cargo area just as the German police arrived to attempt to capture us.

Pilots who successfully escaped and evaded the captors were given time off to go to the Tulip Festival in Amsterdam. As I arrived back at my apartment in Bitburg, I ran in the door and yelled to Elaine, "Pack some clothes. We are going to party in Holland."

MUTUALLY ASSURED
DESTRUCTION

A fter flying at five hundred knots low level, I pulled a four "G" climb while centering the needles on the bomb flight path indicator. Once the rudimentary onboard computer calculated the appropriate release point of the simulated nuclear weapon I was carrying under my F-100 Super Sabre fighter, the bomb automatically disengaged at approximately three thousand feet and arched into the target several miles away,

Theoretically, by lobbing the weapon onto its detonation point, we had time to escape the nuclear blast area before the bomb exploded. We only had enough fuel to reach our assigned target, deliver the weapon, escape the blast and then bail out when the jet engine flamed out (quit). Of course, at that point, numerous nuclear explosions would have taken place throughout Europe in retaliation for attacks on the

Soviet Union. Our survival on foot was going to be short-lived because of the presence of massive amounts of lethal radioactive material covering the ground, produced by the "atomic" and hydrogen bombs.

Basically, our final nuclear attack flight was a Japanese-like *kamikaze* suicide mission to which we had agreed upon our commissioning as officers when we raised our right hands and vowed to protect the Constitution of the United States of America from all enemies; both foreign and domestic.

During the Cold War, generally seen as lasting from 1947 to 1991, both the United States and its NATO Allies were engaged in a very dangerous nuclear deterrent program known as Mutually Assured Destruction (MAD) with the Soviet Union and their Warsaw Pact affiliates.

With each opposing side having tens of thousands of nuclear weapons in their arsenals, the prevailing thought was that no one could possibly survive to retaliate if they were attacked by the other side first. Thus, a worldwide nuclear holocaust would be averted, and total destruction would not occur.

We were practicing nuclear weapon bombing runs for about a month at gunnery ranges located in Libya. In the event of World War III, our fighter aircraft were to be armed with one aerodynamically shaped nuclear weapon, and we would be sent out to bomb the enemy. I was glad we never had to participate in a real nuclear attack because the result would have been the complete and utter destruction of the earth and the end of mankind as we know it.

MUTUALLY ASSURED DESTRUCTION

This is the way the world ends.
This is the way the world ends.
This is the way the world ends.
Not with a bang, but a whimper.

Excerpt from T.S. Elliot,
"The Hollow Men," 1925, T.S. Elliot

RETURN TO THE USA

Before leaving Bitburg, Germany, I went to the base personnel office to inquire about what assignments were available in the United States. The OIC said, "Now that the Korean War is over, there's a surplus of pilots, and you probably need to hide out for a year until assignments stabilize. If you return to the U.S., you will probably be sent to Alaska or Canada as an aircraft controller unit commander located at a radar site along the DEW (Distance Early Warning) line."

The DEW line was an imaginary line running from the northwestern coast of Alaska, in the Aleutian Islands, to the eastern coast of Greenland. Multiple ground-based radar sites were responsible for alerting the USAF in the event Russian bombers attacked North America from the North Pole.

I said, "I really don't want to do that. Are there any other options?"

Thinking for a moment, he answered, "Then, why don't you go back to school for a year?"

I liked that option and applied to Harvard University, Boston, Massachusetts, and was accepted into their School of Advanced Management. However, my plan suddenly changed. Just before I left Germany with Elaine, Bob and Debi, I received a call from my dad telling me that my mother was critically ill with terminal cancer.

Dad was going to take her to the MD Anderson Hospital in Houston, Texas, for chemotherapy treatment. They planned to stay with my sister who lived in nearby Lake Jackson. I called the personnel office and explained the situation. They changed my orders to allow me to go to the University of Texas, located in Austin. The orders further stated, "You are to report to the university and take whatever courses you deem beneficial for your career and the USAF."

Over the next year, I took a total of thirty-nine semester hours and enjoyed taking statistics, economics, manufacturing techniques, and several history courses as electives.

Also attending the university were several former pilots who had worked for me. They were members of the Delta Sigma Pi fraternity, which were primarily students from the management school. Coincidentally, my younger brother and brother-in-law had both been members of the fraternity while attending college.

One day, a member of the fraternity approached me and said, "Carl, we'd like for you to join our fraternity." Six of its members had worked for me, and they decided to "get even" with me. There was nothing vindictive about it; they just thought that it would be fun since I'd been their boss. I accepted their offer to join the group and became the pledge president.

A few days later, I was told we were going to have a party in the hills west of Austin, and the pledges needed to go buy all the food and beer for the event. I asked one of the pledges to go pick up everything and charge it to the Delta Sigma Pi account. All the pledges cut class and met at the ranch—eating all the food and drinking all the beer without the active fraternity members being present.

Of course, when they arrived, there was nothing for them to eat or drink, so they took us to Barton Creek Springs, south of the university campus, threw us in the river and generally harassed us for the rest of the night. They made me wear a dress and vigorously paddled all of us on the butt. The following day, they ordered us to wear Bermuda shorts to class. Afterward, we gathered in a group outside on the steps of the building and loudly sang "I'm So Pretty" from the newly released movie *West Side Story.*

For initiation, they took us to a ranch fifty miles east of Austin and had us take off our boots, low crawl through a muddy pigsty and rub Limburger cheese in our hair. Before all this, they searched us to make sure we didn't have any money. Through my college "intelligence network," I'd learned they were going to chain us to a tree and leave us overnight in a pasture. One of the other pledges was a locksmith, so he took a lock pick and hid it in the cuff of his trousers. At the end of the day, we were all chained to a tree, and the fraternity members departed for Austin. Once the last fraternity member's car's taillights were out of sight, the locksmith opened the locks and freed everybody. We dressed, put on our boots and walked to a light we'd seen across the pasture. As we arrived there, several dogs began barking furiously, and the old rancher came out with a double-barreled shotgun, thinking that we were escaped convicts from the nearby prison.

I yelled, "Don't shoot! We're just a bunch of dumb college students pledging a fraternity."

When he learned we were pledging Delta Sigma Pi, he lowered the gun and said, "That's my fraternity too." His wife made breakfast for us, and we ate outside because we were muddy and smelled bad.

I've been a member of that fraternity for a long time and in 1977, was selected as the Delta Sigma Pi member of the year out of 100,000 total members, a great honor that I cherish.

Upon reporting to the university, I received a letter from Dr. S., who was dean of the management school. He asked me to come to his office, and he told me he had been a World War I fighter pilot in France. He said he would like to be my advisor and sponsor here at the university and did so. He also became a very close friend of mine.

Nine months after my mom and dad moved in with my sister in Lake Jackson, Mom asked to be taken back to Plainview, Texas, because she knew she didn't have much time left to live. A few days after arriving at our home, she passed away. When I was notified of her death, I rented a small airplane and flew into Plainview after refueling in Abilene. I spent a few days and then returned to Austin.

Prior to attending the University of Texas, I had taken night classes at the University of Maryland in Germany and Okinawa. I also had taken classes at the University of Nevada at Las Vegas accumulating one hundred twenty-six semester hours of college credits. I was disappointed to learn that UT only allowed fifty-six of those hours to count toward my degree. I finished my UT courses and then was sent to Luke AFB as Chief of the Standardization and Evaluation Unit for all the instructor pilots. Later, while at Luke, I became the squadron commander of a fighter squadron.

I had a temporary commanding officer (CO) who was a lieutenant colonel, and for some unknown reason didn't like me. He called me into his office one day and said he was assigning me to the academic unit, which was located off the flight line. I moved there and did my best to improve the organization. Soon, I had pilots asking to be transferred to the academic unit as instructors. My CO was upset by my success and wrote on my OER, "This officer should never be promoted beyond major!" In those days, we had to sign the OER, indicating we had reviewed it. I refused to sign and asked to see my CO's boss, the wing commander.

After a lengthy and heated discussion between the two of them, the wing commander, who knew that I had done an outstanding job, ordered my CO to change the OER to all 100s so that the report would not harm my Air Force career.

Many years later, I was playing golf in Arizona with some Air Force buddies. One of them saw my old CO, who had written the bad OER, walk out of the clubhouse. Yelling loudly at him, he said, "Come over here, Lieutenant Colonel H. I'd like to introduce you to Major General Carl Schneider." Revenge, sweet revenge!

UT Campus and Tower

VIETNAM—MAY 1962

"Carl, General Curtis LeMay has personally selected you to go to Vietnam and set up the Air Liaison Officer-Forward Air Controller Program."

I asked, "Where is Vietnam?"

In 1962, Vietnam was virtually an unknown country. My former wing commander, who was now the director of personnel at Tactical Air Command (TAC) laughed and said, "It's what the French call Indochina and it's west of the Philippines. This assignment will be good for your career and speed up your next promotion. This is a highly classified mission because Americans are not supposed to participate in the war between North and South Vietnam."

When I arrived at Clark AFB, located about forty miles northwest of Manila, I reported to the colonel who oversaw the 13th Air Force headquarters. He told me he could get me on an Air Force C-54 flight later that night, going into Tan Son Nhut airport located in Saigon.

After dark, we flew into the airfield, which only had a couple of run down, rusty hangers and one paved runway. After we had exited the airplane, I was the only one left standing on the tarmac after the flight crew and the general, in whose airplane I was flying, departed the airfield. I grabbed my B-4 bag and walked over to a light shining from a Quonset hut. As I walked up to the hut, I saw a Vietnamese soldier asleep in a chair with a rifle lying across his lap.

As I entered the building, I saw all types of office furniture stacked around. At the back, there was a single light bulb hanging from a cord. When I walked up to the desk, I recognized a lieutenant colonel with whom I had worked several years before. He looked up, surprised, and asked, "What are you doing here, Carl?"

I told him that I had been sent there to set up the Forward Air Controller Program.

Standing up, he went to a wall that had a scheduling diagram under a piece of Plexiglas, put my name on it and said, "You can work for me. Let me know when you're through with everything and you can go home."

That meeting was my total orders for the next year that I lived in Vietnam.

I scrounged up all the O-1 Bird-Dog airplanes in the area and recruited thirty-five pilots and crew chiefs to support the operation. One of my pilots was Lt. Thomas McInerney, who went on to become a three-star Air Force Lieutenant General and is frequently a contributor to Fox News.

The name O-1 Bird-Dog was initially chosen because the role of the new aircraft was to find the enemy and circle overhead until artillery (or attack aircraft) could be called in on the enemy, which had been marked with a white phosphorus

2.75-inch folding fin aerial rocket (FFAR) fired by the pilot. When flying low, slow, and close to the battlefield, the pilot was able to observe the enemy targets and adjust the fire using his radios in the manner of a bird-dog used by game hunters.

Flying mainly out of Bien Hoa airbase, located about sixteen miles northeast of Saigon, I always had a Republic of Vietnam Air Force (VNAF) pilot sitting in the backseat. That way, in case I was shot down, I could claim to be an advisor. Any time a FAC pilot went on leave, I temporarily flew in their place, and I saw a lot of South Vietnam from My Tho, Can Tho, Pleiku, Kontum, Hue, Phu Bai, Danang, Chu Lai and Nha Trang.

Many French and German business people remained in Vietnam, and once they found out I was an American major and a USAF fighter pilot, I became somewhat of a VIP and was invited to many formal events. I rented an apartment in Cholon, Saigon, which was the equivalent of Chinatown in Los Angeles in terms of its population and size. I hired a full-time maid who cleaned the place and washed and ironed all my clothes when I came into Saigon. Cholon is a part of Ho Chi Minh City (formerly Saigon) in Vietnam lying on the bank of the Saigon River. It has been long inhabited by Chinese people and is considered the largest Chinatown in the world by area and population.[11]

Many times during the week, I would be flying combat missions or on the ground advising out in the boonies with the South Vietnamese Army, and then I would come back to my apartment to find an engraved invitation to attend concerts, musical performances, and formal dinners at various businessmen's and high-ranking Vietnamese officials' homes.

The maid had my mess dress uniform pressed and laid out for me to wear. I would shower and dress, then go to a soirée and meet with local business people and Vietnamese dignitaries, eat steak and lobster, listen to violin music and drink French wine and champagne. I participated in a very surreal wartime environment.

On Sunday afternoons after chapel services, I went to the Le Cercle Sportif, an exclusive private club built in 1896 for the French colonial society in Saigon. It had a large outdoor swimming pool surrounded by Greek columns and lots of French girls in bikinis. Prominent Americans such as U.S. Ambassador Henry Cabot Lodge, and various South Vietnamese military and political VIP's frequently met at the club. Formal parties, dances, and balls were also held there.

One evening, after a formal dinner party in an old antebellum, American Civil War-style mansion located in the diplomatic area of Saigon, a guard at the front gate let me out, and I started walking down a darkened street to catch a taxi back to my apartment. Suddenly, AK-47s began firing at me, and bullets started ricocheting all around the pavement. I dropped to the ground, but after their magazines were empty, the Vietcong fled the area and I was left alone. I waited a while, quietly lying still on the asphalt and then caught a taxi back to my apartment in Cholon.

Frequently, I worked with the regimental commander of the Army of Vietnam (ARVN) on ground assignments. We ate at sidewalk cafés and little roadside food stands serving all sorts of unrefrigerated food. It was a terrible cultural offense to the Vietnamese if you did not eat with them, so I always did. I'm grateful that it never caused me to have dysentery or sickness in the field. That is until I was preparing to come home from my Vietnam tour and all my subordinates came into Saigon and arranged a party at an exclusive Chinese restaurant in Cholon. The tables had white linen tablecloths, and the waiters all wore tuxedos. Later that night, I got the worst case of dysentery (Nguyen's Revenge) I ever had.

Many times, I traveled north with a group of 5th Special Forces Green Berets, who were constructing encampments, outposts and fire support bases along the Cambodian and Laotian borders. I was setting up their "air request nets" communication systems for them to call in and direct Vietnamese Air Force T-28 attack aircraft to assist in their ground missions.

I also had the privilege to fly with Nguyen Cao Ky, who served as chief of the Vietnam Air Force in the 1960s before leading the nation as its Prime Minister. He relished his flamboyant bad boy image. He wore a black flight suit, dark Ray-Ban sunglasses, a purple scarf, sported a thin mustache, and always smoked a cigarette. On several occasions before his departure from South Vietnam in 1975, I was invited to his home, which was located on the beach in Nha Trang. We had the best lobster I've ever tasted.

When the North Vietnamese communists overran Saigon in 1975, he took his family and flew a helicopter to a U.S. Navy ship and escaped the capture of the city. Settling in Los Angeles, he opened a liquor store, which later failed. Then he tried his hand at the shrimp business in Louisiana but ended up filing bankruptcy for that enterprise as well.

After all my guys and I had been flying for a while, the small arms enemy ground fire increased dramatically whenever we would fly over a hot combat zone. Several times, my pilots had their aircraft badly shot up, and on occasion, the pilots were wounded. When I submitted a request for a medal or decoration, the request was always turned down because the commander did not like paperwork, nor ever wanted to initiate any kind of action. Frustrated at the lack of response, one day, I decided to write a letter "back channels" to General Curtis LeMay. I requested a section be set up properly to award the forward air controller pilots a decoration.

Several weeks later, a full colonel stationed at Hawaii walked into my office and said, "Who is this Major Schneider, and why is he writing through back channels to General LeMay, the Chief of Staff of the Air Force?" My bold, although unauthorized, move was how we were officially able to award Distinguished Flying Crosses, Bronze Stars, Air Medals, and Purple Hearts to the FAC pilots.

One day, the CO of one of the U.S. Army units for whom I had flown called me saying, "Carl, we would like you to come down to Can To (located south of Saigon in the delta) for beer call at our officer's club. We've got a Huey helicopter out at Tan Son Nhut that will bring you down here." Agreeing to the request, I boarded the U.S. Army aircraft, and we flew down to their base.

It was a Friday afternoon, so we all went to their officer's club, which was in an old French mansion with large open windows running three feet from the floor to the ceiling. Because I'd been working closely with them and the FACS, they decided to initiate me into their U.S. Army unit by having me sit in front of the window, while we all drank beer and stacked the cans one on top of each other in front of me.

After several hours, the brigade commander, a colonel, told me how grateful they were for my help and assistance. Unbeknownst to me, staked outside the window was their company mascot—a huge, tame eight-foot tiger that had been defanged and declawed. The person who managed the tiger walked over to me and yelled, "Hoo-Ha," which prompted the tiger to jump through the window and land on my back and shoulders and loudly roar! Of course, I scattered beer cans all over the place trying to escape the beast. The Army officers all began cheering and laughing at my antics.

Before leaving Vietnam, I received orders to the Armed Forces Staff College. I contacted the personnel director, a full colonel, and explained that to further my career, I needed a college degree, and after receiving it, I could then go to the staff college. He agreed and changed my orders sending me to Arizona State University after Vietnam to complete my bachelor's degree—nineteen years after I started at Texas Technological College.

As I was packing up my belongings to return to the United States, I received a call from my boss telling me that Secretary of Defense Robert McNamara, General Curtis LeMay, and several other high-ranking military officers and staff were arriving at Tan Son Nhut airport the next morning and wanted a briefing about what was going on in country. He said, "You have traveled more extensively in country than anyone else, so will you give the briefing to them?"

"Yes, sir, I will," I answered.

Going downtown to Tu Do Street, I went to a store and bought a paper flip chart with an easel stand and some colored markers. I made up a briefing for Defense Secretary McNamara and the other dignitaries. When I finished my presentation, McNamara said, "That was a good briefing, major. What do you think we should do over here?"

Looking directly at him, I said, "Sir, I think we need to immediately bomb all the targets identified around Hanoi, close Haiphong Harbor by mining it and get out of here."

That's what we did ten years later after more than 58,000 American military deaths.

Secretary McNamara jumped up and rushed out the door without saying anything. General LeMay smiled at me with his characteristic cigar in his mouth and gave me a thumbs up as he followed the Secretary of Defense out. Several months later, I was surprised and grateful to be on the lieutenant colonel's promotion list.

General Nguyen Cao Ky

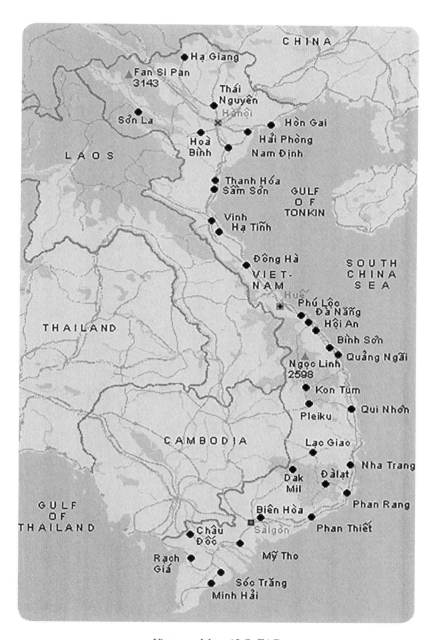

Vietnam Map ALO-FAC

RETURN TO ARIZONA

I was glad to be back in the United States attending Arizona State University and living in Tempe. Elaine was teaching school, and I had just been promoted to lieutenant colonel. After graduating from ASU, we moved to Luke AFB, and I was given an F-100 squadron called the "Top Hats."

One day, while flying with a new second lieutenant pilot riding in the backseat, the tower cleared me to land. When I touched down, I deployed my drogue chute to slow the aircraft. There were two F-100s stopped short and sitting on the taxiway partially blocking the runway on which I had just landed. They had the wrong radio frequency and were unable to talk to ground control and clear the runway.

My aircraft's chute did not deploy properly, nor slow me down, and streamed behind, so at a very high rate of speed, I was forced to steer off the side of the runway to pass the two stationary jets. Then, I quickly got back on the runway, dropped the tail hook, caught the barrier chain and rolled to a stop at the end. I had avoided a major crash that would have destroyed all three jets and killed several pilots with the ensuing inferno caused by igniting jet fuel.

As I was crawling out of the jet, my CO, who saw what had occurred, drove up to me saying, "Carl, you did an amazing job landing the airplane. So, just cool it!"

I was getting ready to go punch the other two pilots in their noses, but he calmed me down. That was one of several times I was almost killed in an airplane. Once again, the Hand of Providence saved my life as He had in Korea after a transport plane I was about to board crashed into the Sea of Japan.

My CO, a brigadier general, called me into his office and said, "Carl, I need you to pack up and go to Fort Riley, Kansas, and check in with the 1st Infantry Division and set up their Tactical Air Control Program."

Being an obedient subordinate, without hesitation, I told him, "Okay, sir."

Once again, our family packed up and moved. We were in Fort Riley two weeks later. After developing the systems to control tactical air support for the "Big Red One" infantry ground units, I went down to Wichita, Kansas, and picked up an F-100 from the Kansas Air National Guard, and let my two ground controllers guide me on to targets at the gunnery ranges. We then switched roles, and I directed them on to the targets also.

Soon, the 1st Infantry Division received orders for Vietnam, and the Army division commander, a two-star major general, called me in and asked me to go with them to Vietnam; because I knew their tactics so well. I called my commander located at Connally AFB in Waco, Texas, and asked if I could fly in and talk to him.

After I had arrived at his office, we discussed this new assignment with the first infantry division. He said he didn't have any replacement for me, so I was going back to Vietnam with them in an advisory ground position. Disappointed, because I wanted to go back to Vietnam as an Air Force F-4 squadron commander, I left his office and was walking down the hall when a sharp looking major walked up and said, "Sir, you don't look very happy."

I replied, "No, I'm not because I'm heading back to Vietnam with the 1st Infantry Division."

Very excitedly, he asked, "Sir, can I have that job, please?"

I grabbed him by the arm, and we walked back into my CO's office, and I said, "Here's my replacement, sir."

After much discussion, he agreed, then turned to me and said, "Well, Carl, what do you want to do now?"

"Sir, I want to go to MacDill AFB in Tampa and take over the Triple Nickel, F-4 squadron and go to Vietnam with them," I answered.

"All right, I'll have your orders cut immediately sending you to Tampa, but first you'll need to go to Tucson to be combat qualified in the F-4 Phantom," he replied.

After qualifying in the F-4, my family and I moved to MacDill AFB into a very small three-bedroom house on base. Originally, I'd planned to move into a larger house on the beach; however, after talking to my new CO and learning that I was going to be working many hours a day, we decided to move into base housing which was closer to my office.

The mission of the 15th wing was changed by the Department of the Air Force (DAF) to train more pilots to become combat ready in the F-4 so they could be sent to Vietnam where there was an extreme shortage of qualified pilots. Because of a lack of training materials, I took a young captain who worked for me. We flew to Luke AFB and then to Nellis AFB requesting their training departments send us instructional materials and training aids which we could use to qualify pilots in the F-4 Phantom.

I was the assistant group operations officer but was practically running the entire operation because of my many flight hours in jet fighters, combat missions in Korea, and extensive combat crew training experience at Luke, Nellis, Pinecastle, and Laughlin AFBs. In six weeks, our team successfully converted the tactical-fighter wing to a training wing. I earned a superior rating (OER) in the process, and I was promoted to full colonel in July.

Arizona State University

MASTER'S DEGREE—
WING CMDR. MOODY AFB

Maxwell AFB is the location of the squadron officer's school for senior lieutenants and captains as well as the Air Command and Staff College for majors and lieutenant colonels. I went to the equivalent Marine Corps school in Quantico, Virginia, instead and then took the Air Command and Staff College course by correspondence. Including the Air War College, these are the three levels of professional education offered by the USAF.

After my assignment in Florida, I attended the Air War College. The course was nine months long and contained intensive material covering a wide range of topics: world affairs, international relations, geopolitical influences, economics, etc. Many times, guest speakers taught the courses.

George Washington University's on-site campus at Maxwell offered a master's degree program on topics related to those the Air War College had in its curriculum. To qualify as a degree for me, the course of study had to be approved by both the Air Force faculty advisor (a full colonel) and on-site professors from the University. The master's program required thirty semester hours to graduate. I completed those courses while I was also taking the Air War College courses and received my master's degree in international relations.

Between the two courses of instructions, I spent approximately eighty hours a week in the library, researching and studying. One month before graduation, I took my completed thesis titled "Indonesia: Economic Impact on Military Potential" to my Air Force advisor who quickly scanned it and then said, "Well, it looks okay for starters and as a first chapter." (In other words, start over!) Before taking it to him, I had met with my George Washington advisor who told me that it looked good but needed a few minor changes. Once those changes were made, the paper was going to be acceptable for the master's degree thesis.

As I walked into my house, I was so mad I threw the paper in the corner of my home office and thought, "To heck with this!"

The next morning when I arrived at school, there was a note in my mailbox telling me that my Air Force advisor had been changed and a new one had been assigned to me. Immediately, I went home, retrieved my thesis and returned to the university to meet the new Air Force advisor. I told him, "My George Washington advisor said that it looks acceptable to him with a couple of minor changes."

The new colonel said, "Well, if it's okay with him, it's okay with me." I left his office breathing a sigh of relief and very happy with the rapid turn of events.

Because I had spent so much time in the library, the librarian knew me by my first name. One morning, she came over to me and whispered, "Carl, there's a Doctor Leonard Marks, Jr. on the phone for you."

Going to the phone, I politely said, "Sir, I don't know who you are, but may I help you?"

He replied, "I'm the Assistant Secretary of the Air Force for Financial Management, and I am looking for an executive officer to manage my office and pilot the T-39 Sabreliner executive jet assigned to me when we travel. I also need someone to oversee my office administration, scheduling, speaking, and social events."

I asked, "Why in the world do you want a dumb old fighter pilot for that job?"

Laughing, he answered, "I'm looking for a colonel with real-world military and combat experience."

After going to his office for an interview, he selected me for the job, and I spent two years working for him in the Pentagon. We flew to approximately one hundred Air Force bases and installations around the world. I piloted the T-39 Sabreliner on domestic flights. On overseas flights, we flew in "Air Force 2", a Boeing 707 which was tasked for special government missions and was a beautifully appointed airplane. Dr. Marks was a great boss and became a long-time friend. He also recommended me for early promotion to general. After two years, I was ready to get back to a normal Air Force flying job, even though the typical job term was four years. Working for Dr. Marks had been a prestigious job; however, I could see that it was limiting my career and promotion advancement.

In my tour in Vietnam, there was a finance officer, Capt. Charlie M, who paid the FAC pilot's their temporary duty (TDY) pay. Walking down the hall in the Pentagon one day, I saw Charlie, now a lieutenant colonel. After visiting with him for a few minutes, I asked if he would be interested in becoming my deputy and he enthusiastically replied, "Yes." He was transferred to me and became my deputy, then my replacement. Later, he ran the Air Force Finance Center and became a major general. After retirement, and for the next ten years, he did an outstanding job as the director of the National Museum of the USAF at Wright-Patterson Air Force Base.

In 1969, after leaving the Pentagon, I was assigned to Moody AFB near Valdosta, Georgia—initially as the director of operations and subsequently the wing commander. Prior to arriving at the base, I received a call from Lieutenant General George B. Simler, who was in charge of the Air Training Command (ATC).

He said, "Do you want that wing at Moody?"

I quickly answered, "Yes, sir."

"Then if you do a good job as the director of operations, I'll try to get you promoted to wing commander and brigadier general. If you don't do a good job, I'll fire your butt!"

Hesitatingly, I asked, "Boss, can I say something?"

"What's that?" he said.

"I want you to stay off my back and don't send your staff down to Moody questioning my methods or motives for anything that I do. If you do that, I promise you we will have the best wing in your command."

A year and a half later, I called him and laughingly said, "Boss, I'm tired of your supervision. You called me one time. You wrote me one letter, and you came to see me one time." That was my total supervision from Lieutenant General Simler and, true to his word, I was promoted.

He recommended my promotion to brigadier general. I was the first colonel to be promoted to general while stationed at Moody AFB as the wing commander since 1942. After my promotion, almost all the wing commanders at Moody were ultimately promoted to general officers. Recently, the Chief of Staff of the Air Force, a four-star general, was promoted from Moody Air Force Base while serving as the commander.

The United States Senate confirmed my promotion, and soon I was sent to briefings from generals in the Air Force, Army, Marines, and Navy admirals about how to be a general officer. The State Department also had high-ranking officials who addressed us during the orientation.

The only talk that I can remember was when the Chief of Staff of the Air Force walked in late one day and said, "Okay, guys, don't get a big head because there are fifty colonels out there just as good as you. You've all had tough jobs and deserved to be promoted. But don't think that you're any better than anybody else. There are no bad jobs for generals. There's more work than you can possibly get done in any assignment, so don't politic for any job. We will tell you where we need you to go. Also, expect some subordinates to fail and disappoint you. Just accept it and deal with it." Pausing for just a minute, he said, "If you don't like it, quit and go do something else." Then he walked out the door.

Future President Lieutenant George W. Bush went through flight school at Moody AFB from November 25, 1968, to November 28, 1969. I was in the process of being promoted to wing commander from director of operations. His mother, Barbara, and father, George H.W. Bush, came to visit him twice while he was in training, and I had dinner with both parents and "Junior." I think his mother was the funniest woman I've ever met. They were just great folks—very sincere and down to earth.

Lieutenant Bush graduated in the top part of his class, and although he wasn't a class appointed leader, he had charisma, and his classmates gravitated to him. While in flight school, he flew twin-engine T-37 Tweets and T-38 Talons.

As director of operations, I went to Perrin AFB near Dallas, Texas and got checked out to be an instructor pilot in T-37s before reporting to Moody. I usually flew two or three times per week with students to maintain my proficiency as an instructor. When I was promoted to wing commander, I had the Moody AFB chief instructor pilot for T-38s qualify me as an instructor in them too, so I was flying both aircraft as an instructor.

General Simler's one phone call to me began with, "Carl, as director of operations, Air Force regulations require you to be qualified in the T-37."

I replied, "Yes, sir. I am."

"But now that you are the wing commander you have to be qualified in the T-38," he said.

"Yes, sir. I'm qualified in the T-38 too," I replied.

Pausing for a moment, General Simler said, "I wish all my wing commanders would get off their butts and work like you do. Then I could play golf all day long." He abruptly hung up.

George Bush as a Student Pilot

George Bush by a T-38 Talon

RETURN TO KOREA

After I had arrived at Osan AFB in Korea as a newly promoted brigadier general, I was assigned as the Vice Commander of all the Air Force, NATO, and Republic of Korea aviation assets in Korea. When I had left San Francisco that morning, I was a full colonel, but I'd been instructed to have a flight attendant pin on my first star in route so that when I landed, I would outrank my Army counterparts. This was an important factor in the U.S. military hierarchy of Korea because most of the commanders were in the U.S. Army.

Shortly after arriving, the air division commander walked into my office and announced that he was returning to the United States for back surgery to repair an injury he had sustained after ejecting from an F-4 Phantom jet in Vietnam. For the next four months, I was the acting air division commander for all USAF units in Korea. When my commander returned, he told me that he was going to retire and that I was going to be "frocked" (temporarily promoted) to a two-star general (major general) which the position required. "But, Carl you can't bring your family over here," he informed me.

Somewhat disgruntled, I said, "In that case, sir, I can't accept the position, because I promised my daughter when she was eight years old that I would make sure she spent the last two years of high school in one location. She has never gone to the same school for two consecutive years due to our frequent assignments. What are my other options?"

Thinking a moment, he said, "You can move up North to Seoul where there are beautiful family quarters, and your daughter can go to the Seoul American School, but you won't be promoted to major general."

"Then I'll take it, sir." I quickly said.

He also told me, "In that job, you'll also be the longest-serving brigadier general in history."

In the span of one conversation, I went from the fastest promotion to the slowest. When I was finally promoted to major general, I was the one with the longest time in grade as a brigadier. Our daughter, Debi, graduated with honors from her high school where many children of diplomats also attended.

In Seoul, my USAF staff and I were responsible for overseeing all the exercises necessary to prevent and repel a North Korean attack and invasion across the Demilitarized Zone (DMZ). Additionally, I had another group called the "US/ROK" (Republic of Korea) Operational Planning Staff that ran ongoing computer simulations of the tactical air defenses and logistical requirements of a possible war with North Korea.

As my position was officially recognized by all the various NATO Allies' embassies, my wife and I were required to attend many social functions each week. Frequently, when high-ranking Air Force personnel visited Seoul, Elaine entertained the ladies at our house and then took them shopping downtown. She did a magnificent job as the only Air Force general's wife in Korea.

My senior CO was a U.S. Army four-star, General Richard G. Stilwell, no relation to "Vinegar Joe Stilwell." He had a turboprop Beechcraft A-90 King Air, designated as the U-21 Ute, assigned to him to fly around Korea. He rarely used the airplane. One day, I went into his office and said, "Boss, I'm flying all over Korea and occasionally to Japan checking on various exercises and could use your U-21 to get into some of the airfields. If you let me use it, I'll make sure that it's fully gassed and ready to go anytime you need it." He agreed, and after getting checked out in the turboprop, I frequently flew his plane, amassing three hundred hours flying time in the aircraft.

Several years earlier after my combat tour in Korea, a group of twelve Korean fighter pilots came to the United States to learn how to fly T-33 jets. Their senior officer was Captain Ach Min Ho. I was their instructor pilot and taught them all how to fly the jet. Twenty years later, the captain was now a four-star general, Chief of Staff of the Korean Air Force, and all the lieutenants were two-star generals.

General Ach Min Ho had a big party for us the night after Elaine and I arrived in Korea and told me that I could fly any aircraft in the Korean Air Force, saying, "You can go down to Taegu and fly F-4s or go to Kimpo and fly F-86s, or you can go to Suwon and fly F-5s." I had a lot of time in the T-38 which is the training version of the F-5 fighter. Excited about the possibility, I had a driver pick me up the next morning, and we drove to Suwon.

Arriving at base headquarters, I met the wing commander who was a Korean brigadier general whom I did not know. I explained that I was going to fly one of their F-5s as authorized by General Ach Min Ho.

He said, "Ah so." He had a young Korean major, who spoke English, come to his office and brief me about the aircraft. Then, the wing commander called the general in Seoul who authorized my check out in the airplane.

The young major said, "General, how much time do you have flying in the F-5?"

I answered, "None."

Not saying anything, he nodded his head, and we walked out to the flight line where I climbed into the front seat. "General, maybe you should fly in the back seat," he said.

"No. I want to fly in the front seat." I answered.

About that time the wing commander drove up in a staff car, and he and the major had a heated discussion in Korean. The major came back and said, "The general thinks you need to fly in the back seat!"

Emphatically I said, "No. I'm flying in the front seat. Now let's go."

We took off, and I flew different aerobatic maneuvers, stalls, and touch-and-go landings. Finally, entering the traffic pattern, I landed and taxied up to base operations. In my rearview mirror (which allowed me to see the major), I saw him smile big and give the "OK" sign to the wing commander, who was sitting by the runway in his staff car watching my flight. From then on during my tour, I was fully welcome to fly with the Korean Air Force and was honored to receive the ROKAF pilot wings.

Frequently, I received a phone call in the middle of the night from one of my former Korean jet students, who was now my counterpart in the Korean Air Force, informing me that the President of Korea, Park Chung-Hee wanted to launch the Air Force fighters to go shoot at North Korean boats that had illegally entered South Korean waters. We were driven in a staff car to the "Blue House" (the equivalent of the White House) where we had to convince President Park not to start a major war over a few fishing boats inside his territorial waters.

Before leaving Korea for my next assignment in the United States, I was attending a cocktail party one evening when I met the commander of the Air Force Logistics Command, who was touring the Asian Pacific Rim. Coming up to me, he asked, "After your tour is up in Korea where are you being assigned, Carl?"

I answered, "Sir, I'll go wherever the general officers' shop sends me."

After explaining his organization's mission, he asked, "How would you like to work for me in logistics? I'm looking for some young brigadiers who will become vice commanders for air logistics centers throughout the Air Force. If you do a good job, we will promote you to major general and give you an air logistics center to run. I've checked you out and know that you went to the University of Texas advanced industrial management program, so I think you'll be perfect for the job."

I said, "Sounds good to me, sir." So, when my Korean tour was completed, Elaine, Debi, and I returned to the United States and moved back to Georgia.

Carl in Seoul, Korea with UN Command

LOGISTICS COMMAND

After I had arrived at Warner Robins AFB, I became the Air Logistics Vice Commander. The base is located approximately eighteen miles south of Macon, Georgia. Now called Robins AFB, it is home to one of the U.S. Air Force materiel commands air logistics centers. The others are the Oklahoma City Air Logistics Center at Tinker AFB and Ogden Air Logistics Center at Hill AFB in Utah.

When I arrived at Robins, I found that most of the personnel were federal employees who had worked in logistics for many years. One day, I went to the main supervisor and asked, "Who knows more about logistics in this place than anybody else?"

He answered, "That's Hal C. for sure. He started here years ago as a GS-1 when they first opened the base, and now he is a GS-17."

I called Hal and introduced myself. Then I said, "I need you to teach me everything you can about logistics."

He replied, "General you come down to my office each morning at 7:00 a.m., Monday through Friday, for the next three months, and I'll teach you everything you need to know about logistics."

I arrived at his office early the next morning. He closed and locked the door, then went to a blackboard and slowly wrote; *L-O-G-I-S-T-I-C-S* on it. Over the next three months, I explored every nook, cranny, and office on the base observing all the workings of the air logistics program.

One year after arriving at Robins, I was promoted to major general. We moved to Tinker AFB in Oklahoma City where I became the commander of the air logistics center there. It is the worldwide manager for the B-52 bomber, KC-135 refueling aircraft, and A-7 fighter. Tinker also handles engines, software, missiles, weapon systems, avionics, and accessories.

Carl at Warner Robins as Brigadier General

CHIEF OF STAFF USAF
LOGISTICS COMMAND

My predecessor at Tinker AFB was a very intelligent two-star general who was trying to do everything by himself instead of trusting the job to the highly qualified civilian federal employees. Once he left, I took over. Each day found several supervisors lined up outside my office needing approval for lots of "nickel and dime" decisions which they were perfectly capable of making for themselves.

I decided everyone needed to be retrained to make their own decisions. I went to four of the universities located in Oklahoma and convinced the presidents to send me several of their top professors in industrial management, engineering, and business psychology to help me develop a training program for my staff.

We put together a two-week program that included a class of two senior managers, three mid-level managers, and fifteen first line supervisors without their immediate bosses so they were free to talk and express themselves without fear of retaliation. This built a very close, cohesive team.

The classes were held off base so there wasn't any interference from any work-related issues that might arise. The program was so successful that it is still in existence today and is run the same way with appropriate updates. It was nicknamed the Superman Program, which gave my staff plenty of opportunities to joke with me about the name Superman and my role as the Super Hero.

I remained at Tinker AFB for approximately one year and then moved to Wright-Patterson AFB in Dayton, Ohio, where I became the Chief of Staff of the Air Force Logistic Command. I implemented several new programs to better support our operational commands. After a year in that assignment, I chose to retire with thirty-two wonderful years in the USAF. My wife, Elaine, and I then moved to Arizona.

My childhood dream of becoming a fighter pilot and flying jet aircraft had been ultimately fulfilled. I look back upon my career with immense pride, gratitude, and awe at how everything unfolded. Imagine entering the U.S. Army Air Force in 1946 as an enlisted private and thirty-two years later, in 1978, leaving the USAF as a major general. I have been a mightily blessed man and believe that Divine Providence has guided my entire life.

A-7 Pilot

A-7 Pilot Climbing Down Ladder

A-7 Pilot

Standing at Podium

Tinker AFB Change of Command

Superman

A-7 Pilot

USAF 2 Star

POSTLUDE

As it began to lightly snow, I started my car and drove out of the Wright-Patterson AFB parking lot of what was now my former office building and returned to the hotel where Elaine and I planned to spend the night before starting our journey to our new home in Phoenix, Arizona. After loading the car early the next morning, we drove to nearby Interstate 70 and began heading west. From Dayton, Ohio, to our new home was 1,815 miles—a distance I wistfully remembered I could fly in about three hours in an Air Force F-4 Phantom. However, we expected to drive approximately five hundred to six hundred miles each day until we reached our destination in three or four days.

At St. Louis, we began driving on the Historic Route 66 and stayed on it for most of the trip to Flagstaff, Arizona. There we drove south on Interstate 17 into Phoenix. Driving cross country along Route 66, Elaine and I felt like kids on a new adventure. We enjoyed the vast scenery even though it was cold and wintry along the way. When we arrived in Phoenix, we were glad to reach our destination and anxious to begin life in our new home. We lived there happily for twenty-one years until Elaine died in 1999.

After two years, I married Carole and began an exciting new chapter in life with her. For many years now, I've been involved in helping student veterans enrolled in colleges and universities in Arizona and Tennessee since retiring from the USAF.

Carole and Carl at Pima, AZ Hall of Fame

AWARDS AND DECORATIONS

The Distinguished Service Medal
The Legion of Merit with Oak Leaf Cluster
The Distinguished Flying Cross with Oak Leaf Cluster
The Meritorious Service Medal
The Air Medal with six Oak Leaf Clusters
The Air Force Commendation Medal
Numerous other miscellaneous medals and awards

MY CIVILIAN CAREER

Since my retirement in 1978, I've been actively engaged in many volunteer opportunities to help military veterans, my community, and our country. While living in Arizona, I began by volunteering with the Joe Foss Institute, established to improve the knowledge of students on the importance of the U.S. Constitution and the Bill of Rights.

As a board member, I gave presentations to schools throughout Arizona, addressing approximately five thousand students. Traveling to Georgia, I provided eight briefings to various school systems throughout the state. In an effort to expand the program to other states, I traveled to Nevada, New Mexico, Ohio, Texas, and Florida to recruit veterans to volunteer with the organization.

In 2007, I was selected as one of eight Korean War veterans to travel to the Republic of South Korea as a diplomatic/military representative. As an envoy, I provided consultation as a highly-regarded representative of that country and received the "Ambassador for Peace Award" from the Republic of Korea government.

I'm a member of many military and fraternal organizations including the Military Officers Association of America (MOAA), the Air Force Association, Daedalions, the Knights of the Round Engine, the Arizona Aviation Historical Society, Quiet Birdman, Experimental Aircraft Association (EAA), and many other groups. I've also been inducted into the Arizona Aviation Hall of Fame and the Arizona Veterans Hall of Fame.

I've also been involved in numerous successful business ventures. Most of my activities have included working with veterans and assisting with their efforts to obtain comprehensive healthcare and launch new businesses. Currently I am the president of the Veteran's Resource Group located in Tennessee.

HIGH FLIGHT

JOHN GILLESPIE MCGEE JR

"Oh! I have slipped the surly bonds of earth,
And danced the skies on laughter-silvered wings;
Sunward I've climbed and joined the tumbling mirth
Of sun-split clouds, and done a hundred things
You have not dreamed of –
Wheeled and soared and swung
High in the sunlit silence.
Hovering there
I've chased the shouting wind along
and flung
my eager craft through footless halls of air …
Up, up the long, delirious, burning blue,
I've topped the wind-swept heights with easy grace,
Where never lark or even eagle, flew;
And, while with silent, lifting mind I've trod
The high untrespassed sanctity of space,
Put out my hand and touched the face of God."

RECOMMENDED BOOK READING LIST

1. *The Holy Bible*
2. *No Dream is Too High*—Dr. Buzz Aldrin, ScD.
3. *Vietnam Saga*—Stan Corvin, Jr.
4. *Little House on the High Plains*—Major General Carl G. Schneider, USAF (Ret.)

APPENDIX

In my thirty-two-year career, I experienced tremendous changes in the USAF. World War II in the Pacific Rim ended on September 2, 1945, after Japan surrendered. Germany had already surrendered on May 8, 1945, ending the war in Europe. Military demobilization began near the latter part of 1945, and hundreds of thousands of soldiers, sailors, airmen, and Marines were sent home. Many war brides needed to be processed through immigration for American citizenship.

The War Assets Administration was responsible for disposing of a massive amount of equipment, supplies, and airplanes. Sixty thousand aircraft, some just off the final assembly line in a manufacturing plant, in preparation for the anticipated invasion of Japan, were sent to scrap yards where they were cut up and destroyed.

Huge aircraft storage facilities were created in the western deserts of Arizona, Texas, and California, and thousands of airplanes were mothballed in those locations; many are still there after having been cannibalized for parts.

The United States Army Air Force (USAAF) officially became the United States Air Force (USAF) in September 1947. A Reduction in Force (RIF) was instituted for all the military personnel, and many were given the order, "Pack up today and go home."

Some of the best officers and NCOs left the service, while many of the lesser-qualified remained. It took many years to rebuild a quality military force. Many of the remaining pilots were grounded and told to work in other areas, such as supply officers counting sheets and/or painting fence posts until more jet aircraft were available. The Defense Department's budget was slashed by Secretary of Defense Louis Johnson, who believed there was no need for a big military force in the peacetime world. His decision resulted in massive shortages of aviation parts and equipment; e.g., helmets; gloves, flight suits, oxygen masks, etc.

During the early years of jet aviation, new tactics and procedures were slowly being developed and incorporated into the training of the pilots. An example was the teardrop letdown (reversing course) IFR approach which allowed pilots to land safely in bad weather and maintain terrain avoidance, which previously was the cause of many airplane accidents. Early cross-country flights were navigated using "dead reckoning" calculations (time, distance and heading) because of inadequate flight instruments in the airplanes.

The E6B flight computer (nicknamed the "whiz wheel"), resembling a circular slide rule, was utilized by virtually all pilots, both military and civilians. Today, with sophisticated global positioning system (GPS) receivers, pilots can know the take-off heading, distance, and time to their destination before ever leaving their initial ground position on a parking ramp.

Once, while flying cross country in an F-100, my canopy broke, and I was forced to land at a nearby airport. The frigid air blowing in the cockpit nearly froze me to death because I was wearing only a thin flight suit and jacket. Because of the thermodynamics phenomenon called adiabatic cooling, the temperature drops approximately three degrees (called the lapse rate) for each thousand feet of flight altitude. Usually, the outside air temperature (OAT) at 35,000 feet was one hundred five degrees colder than the ground. Frequently, in winter the temperature at that altitude was eighty degrees below zero.

I flew jet aircraft for over ten years before the first commercial airliner (a Boeing 707) was certified to carry passengers in 1959. On cross-country flights, the superior performance characteristics of the jet fighter allowed me to climb to 35,000 feet en route to my destination and watch the slower propeller-driven airliners flying well below me.

While flying all alone at night, I frequently was in awe of the crystal-clear sky above my canopy filled with a multitude of stars—an absolutely beautiful and a stunning display of earth's wondrous creation.

The heavens declare the glory of God;
the skies proclaim the work of His hands.
—Psalm 19 NIV

LIFE'S LESSONS I'VE LEARNED

- A positive "can do" attitude is essential for success.
- Innovation and hard work are necessary.
- A vision for your organization is required.
- Common sense in all things is a necessity.
- Asking many questions and listening carefully to the replies is important.
- Frequent unit visits are critical.
- Calculated risk takers and success stories should be celebrated.
- Key people should be chosen carefully and then allowed to make decisions in their unit.
- "Develop your God-given talents, balance your goals, work smart, work hard and enjoy life; it has an expiration date!"

ENDNOTES

1. *www.thegreatdepression.com/dust_bowl*
2. *www.millercenter.org/president/speeches/JFK*
3. *www.lowryfoundation.org/lowry.afb/*
4. *www.wfbmuseum.org/history-of-walker-air-force-base/*
5. *www.military.com/base-guide/randolph-air-force-base*
6. *www. shaw.af.mil/history*
7. *www.War in the Skies, Korean Conflict June 1950-July 1953.*
8. *www.itazuke.org/history*
9. *www.usafpolice.org/Korea/Kimpo.html*
10. *www.faa.gov/about/history/radar_departure_control. pdf*
11. *www.chinatownology.com/chinatown_cholon.html*

TABLE OF ABBREVIATIONS

AB	Air Base
AETC	Air Education and Training Command
AFB	Air Force Base
AFPC	Air Force Personnel Center
AG	Above ground level
AO	Area of operations
ARVN	Army of Vietnam
ASU	Arizona State University
ATC	Air Training Command
AWOL	Absent Without Leave
BG	Brigadier General
BOQ	Bachelor officers' quarters
CAVU	Ceiling and Visibility Unlimited
CO	Commanding officer
DAF	Department of the Air Force
DEW	Distance Early Warning
DMZ	Demilitarized Zone

TABLE OF ABBREVIATIONS

E&E	Escape and Evasion
EAA	Experimental Aircraft Association
FAC	Forward Air Controller
FACS	Forward air controllers
FFAR	Folding fin aerial rocket
FTX	Field Training Exercises
GCA	Ground Control Approach
GPS	Global positioning system
IFR	Instrument Flight Rules
IG	Inspector General
KPAF	Korean People's Air Force
LTC	Lieutenant Colonel
MAD	Mutually Assured Destruction
MASH	Mobile Army Surgical Hospitals
MiG	Russian and Chinese Swept-wing Jet
MIT	Massachusetts Institute of Technology
MOAA	Military Officers Association of America
NATO	North Atlantic Treaty Organization
NCO	Non-Commissioned Officer (enlisted person)
OAT	Outside air temperature
OER	Officers' effectiveness report
OIC	Officer in charge
PCS	Permanent change of station
POW	Prisoner of War
PTSD	Post-traumatic stress disorder
RIF	Reduction in Force
ROKAF	Republic of Korea Air Force
ROTC	Reserve Officer Training Corp
SAC	Strategic Air Command
ScD	Doctor of Science
TAC	Tactical Air Command

TDY	Temporary Duty
TOT	Time over target
USAAF	United States Army Air Force
USAA	United Services Automobile Association
USAFE	United States Air Forces Europe
USAF	United States Air Force
USS	United States Ship
US	United States
VHF	Very High Frequency
VNAF	(South)Vietnam Air Force
WWI	World War One
WWII	World War Two

55077052R00104

Made in the USA
Columbia, SC
10 April 2019